Create Stunning Animations Using Corona and V-Ray in 3ds Max

This book is a step-by-step guide on how to create realistic animations using Corona and V-Ray within 3ds Max. It caters to beginners and intermediate users, helping them transform static renders into dynamic and captivating animations. It combines technical knowledge with practical examples, covering everything from basic principles to advanced techniques.

By the end of this book, readers will:

- Understand the fundamentals of animation in 3ds Max.
- Learn to animate cameras, objects, and lights effectively.
- Create realistic animated scenes using Corona and V-Ray.
- Explore time-saving workflows and rendering optimization tips.
- Develop a polished animation portfolio ready for professional projects.

This book is structured as a nuts-and-bolts how-to guide, breaking down complex animation techniques into manageable steps. Each chapter focuses on a specific aspect of animation, blending foundational knowledge with advanced tips to enhance the reader's understanding and capability. Through detailed explanations, visual examples, and step-by-step tutorials, this book aims to demystify the animation process for beginners while offering advanced insights for experienced users.

Margarita Nikita is the co-founder of High Q Renders LLC, an award-winning creative company based in San Francisco, CA, and with offices in Greece. Nikita has published several design books on 2D and 3D graphic design, some of which are used in university courses, actively contributing to the formation of the new generations of 3D modelers in her native country, Greece. Nikita has created a YouTube channel to share her knowledge, advice, and tips and tricks. Visit her Instagram account, margarita.nikita, to see more of her work.

Create Stunning Animations Using Corona and V-Ray in 3ds Max

Guiding the Next Generation of 3D Renderers

Margarita Nikita

CRC Press
Taylor & Francis Group
Boca Raton London New York

CRC Press is an imprint of the
Taylor & Francis Group, an **Informa** business

Designed cover image: Shutterstock

First edition published 2026
by CRC Press
2385 NW Executive Center Drive, Suite 320, Boca Raton FL 33431

and by CRC Press
4 Park Square, Milton Park, Abingdon, Oxon, OX14 4RN

CRC Press is an imprint of Taylor & Francis Group, LLC

ISBN: 9781041096702 (hbk)
ISBN: 9781041096672 (pbk)
ISBN: 9781003651222 (ebk)

DOI: 10.1201/9781003651222

Typeset in Minion
by codeMantra

To my sons,

Vaggelis and Konstantinos,

*always remember: the most magical animations
start with a single keyframe.*

And to my parents,

Panos and Mata,

*who set the first keyframe in my life, giving me the direction,
and the confidence to bring my dreams to life.*

Contents

Acknowledgments   x

1 Getting Started   1

1.1   3ds Max Interface Overview 1
1.2   Viewports 4
1.3   Create and Modify Standard Primitives 9
1.4   Selecting Objects 13
1.5   Transform Commands 14
     1.5.1   Select and Move 14
     1.5.2   Select and Rotate 16
     1.5.3   Select and Scale 17
     1.5.4   Select and Place 18
1.6   Saving a Project 19
     1.6.1   Save As 19
     1.6.2   Save Selected 20
     1.6.3   Archive... 20

2 Animation Basics in 3ds Max   21

2.1   Introduction to Animation Controls..21
     2.1.1   The Time Slider and Track Bar..21
     2.1.2   The Animation Controls 22
2.2   Animation Settings... 24
     2.2.1   What Is a Frame?... 24
     2.2.2   Frame Rate 24
     2.2.3   Time Display 26
     2.2.4   Playback 27

	2.2.5	Animation	28
	2.2.6	Examples...	29
2.3		Getting Started with Keyframes	29
	2.3.1	What Is a Keyframe?....................................	29
	2.3.2	Auto Key vs. Set Key	30
	2.3.3	Examples..	30
	2.3.4	Step-by-Step Example: Animating a Box with Auto Key	30
	2.3.5	Step-by-Step Example: Animating a Sphere with Set Key..	32
	2.3.6	Adjusting Keyframes for Timing........................	35
	2.3.7	Copying Keyframes for Repeated Motion..........	35
	2.3.8	Deleting Keyframes from the Timeline..............	36
2.4		Animating Parameters.....................................	38
	2.4.1	Step-by-Step Example: Animating the Height of the Box..	38
	2.4.2	Step-by-Step Example: Animating the Hemisphere Value of a Sphere	39
2.5		Animating Modifiers..	40
	2.5.1	Step-by-Step Example: Animating the Bend Modifier	40
	2.5.2	Step-by-Step Example: Animating the Skew Modifier	41
2.6		Curves...	43
	2.6.1	Accessing the Curve Editor	43
	2.6.2	Overview of the Curve Editor	43
	2.6.3	Step-by-Step Example: Adjusting the Box's X-Position Curve	44
	2.6.4	Understanding Ease In and Ease Out	44
	2.6.5	Choosing the Right Motion	45

3 Camera Animation   46

3.1		Simple Camera Animation.................................	46
	3.1.1	Animating the Position of the Camera..............	46
	3.1.2	Animating the Position of the Camera and the Camera Target	49
	3.1.3	Animating the Camera Using the Camera Navigation Controls....................	55
3.2		Animating the Camera Settings.........................	57
	3.2.1	Step-by-Step Example: Animating the Camera Focal Length	58
	3.2.2	Step-by-Step Example: Animating Camera Clipping.......	60
	3.2.3	Step-by-Step Example: Animating Depth of Field (DoF)...	62

3.3   Walkthrough 68
        3.3.1   · Step-by-Step Example: Creating a Walkthrough
                Animation 69

4 Lighting Animation   80

4.1   Light Intensity Animation.. 80
        4.1.1   Step-by-Step Example: Animating the Intensity
                of the Pendant... 80
        4.1.2   Step-by-Step Example: Animating the Intensity
                of the Pendant Lights... 83
4.2   Color Temperature and Light's Color Animation 88
        4.2.1   Step-by-Step Example: Animating the Color
                Temperature of the Pendants 88
        4.2.2   Step-by-Step Example: Animating a Light's Color
                Change 90
4.3   Sunlight Animation.. 93
        4.3.1   Step-by-Step Example: Animating the Position
                of the Sun.. 93

5 Rendering Settings for Animation   97

5.1   Understanding the Rendering Workflow............................... 97
        5.1.1   Step-by-Step Rendering Workflow 97
5.2   Rendering Settings in Corona... 100
5.3   Rendering Settings in V-Ray... 101
5.4   Combining Images into a Movie... 106
5.5   Rendering Using Chaos Cloud 112
5.6   Topaz Labs 113
        5.6.1   Step-by-Step Example: Using Topaz Video AI
                to Upscale a Video... 114
        5.6.2   Step-by-Step Example: Using Topaz Video AI
                to Combine Images into a Video 118
        5.6.3   Step-by-Step Example: Using Topaz Video AI for
                Frame Interpolation... 120

6 Simulations   123

6.1   Installing Chaos Phoenix 123
6.2   Water Faucet Simulation 124
        6.2.1   Step-by-Step Example: Faucet Water Simulation........... 126
6.3   Fireplace Simulation.. 140
        6.3.1   Step-by-Step Example: Fireplace Fire Simulation 141

Index   157

Acknowledgments

To everyone who read my previous books, *Create Stunning Renders Using V-Ray in 3ds Max* (CRC Press, 2021) and *Create Stunning Renders Using Corona in 3ds Max* (CRC Press, 2024) – your feedback and enthusiasm keep me going. This book on animation in Corona and V-Ray is for you.

To my Udemy students and YouTube subscribers – your curiosity, questions, and wins have shaped this book more than you know.

To my amazing team at HighQ Renders – thank you for turning static scenes into stories and for inspiring many of the exercises in this book.

To Dimitris Batis of Batis Studio for always pushing me to refine my workflow. Your daily support means a lot.

And to my sons, Vaggelis and Konstantinos – your imagination is a reminder that the real magic isn't just in animation, but in the way we see the world.

My Story

My early days as a renderer remind me of my first time at the gym. I walked in full of motivation, but after 10 minutes on the treadmill, I was exhausted and questioned everything.

3D rendering and animation are a lot like building muscle – it takes daily effort, and at first, it's tough. But with consistency, it becomes second nature. For the record, I still struggle at the gym. But rendering? That's a different story.

Fast forward 18 years, and I'm the co-founder of HighQ Renders LLC, an award-winning creative studio based in San Francisco, with offices in Greece. In 2023 and 2024, I was honored to be named in the Fortune Greece 40 Under 40, and in 2024, HighQ Renders was recognized among the 100 Fastest Growing Companies in San Francisco.

Our portfolio includes some of the most iconic projects in the world – Fontainebleau Las Vegas, Marriott Hotels & Resorts in New York, Hilton

Hotels in New York, Ritz-Carlton Residences in Miami, and Hyatt in New York – along with collaborations with celebrity designers like Kari Whitman and Fox Nahem, whose clients include Barack Obama, Jessica Alba, Melanie Griffith, and Robert Downey Jr.

Beyond client work, I've published multiple books on 2D and 3D design, some of which are used in universities to train the next generation of 3D artists. I also share my knowledge through my YouTube channel and Udemy courses, helping creatives sharpen their skills in rendering and animation.

If you're just starting out, my goal is to guide you. From workflows and rendering settings to working with clients and growing your business, I'll share everything I've learned – from being a solo freelancer to leading a growing 19-member team.

This book is for architects, interior designers, 3D artists, and anyone eager to explore animation in Corona and V-Ray for 3ds Max. No prior animation experience is required, but a basic understanding of 3ds Max will help.

We'll go beyond static renders to bring scenes to life – learning camera movements, motion rendering settings, dynamic lighting, and storytelling through animation. Step by step, you'll build and animate a small interior project, with downloadable resources to follow along.

This book is tailored to Corona 12, V-Ray 7, and 3ds Max 2025. Whether you're taking your first steps in animation or refining your skills, I hope it inspires you to bring your vision to life – one frame at a time.

Yours,
Margarita Nikita

1

Getting Started

1.1 3ds Max Interface Overview

When you open Autodesk 3ds Max 2025, a Welcome Screen appears. It is a set of slides designed to provide new users with basic information to help get started (Figure 1.1).

When you close the Welcome Screen, you see the 3ds Max interface (Figure 1.2), which consists of the following items:

1. **Title bar:**
   It shows the name of the project and the version of the 3ds Max. Every new project is named by default Untitled, and you need to Save the project to rename it (see Section 1.6).

2. **Menu bar (File, Edit, Tools, etc.):**
   It contains drop-down menus with commands. The name of each menu indicates the purpose of the commands.

3. **Main Toolbar:**
   It provides quick access to some of the most used commands in 3ds Max, like Undo, Redo, Move, Rotate, or Scale.

DOI: 10.1201/9781003651222-1

Figure 1.1

Welcome Screen in Autodesk 3ds Max 2025.

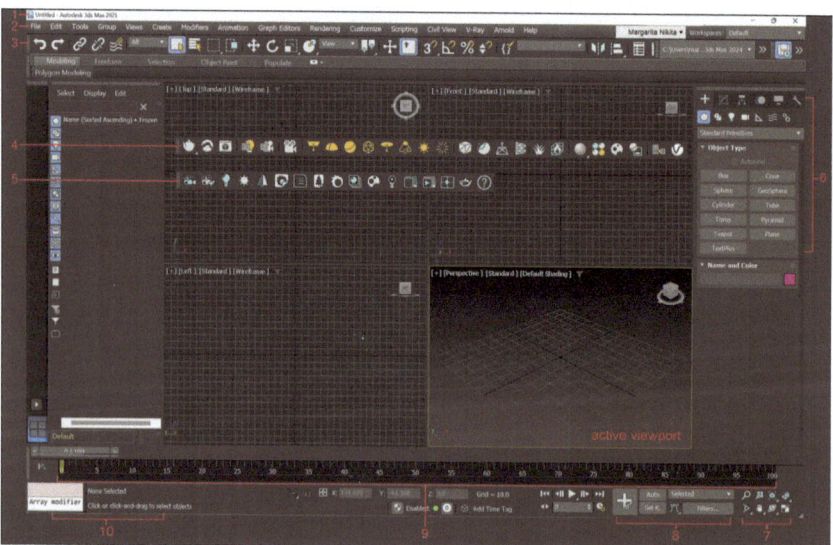

Figure 1.2

Autodesk 3ds Max 2025 interface.

4. **V-Ray Toolbar:**

It contains shortcuts for some of the most used V-Ray commands. For more information on V-Ray, please see the book *Create Stunning Renders Using V-Ray in 3ds Max: Guiding the Next Generation of 3D Renderers.*

5. **Chaos Corona Toolbar:**

It contains shortcuts for some of the most used Corona commands. For more information on Corona, please see the book *Create Stunning Renders Using Corona in 3ds Max: Guiding the Next Generation of 3D Renderers.*

6. **Command Panel:**

It consists of six sub-panels: Create, Modify, Hierarchy, Motion, Display, and Utilities. They include controls for creating objects, editing them, animation and display options, and miscellaneous utilities. You use this panel mainly to create and edit the cameras and the lights in a scene.

7. **Viewport Navigation Controls:**

It includes buttons that control the display and navigation of the viewports. Some of the buttons change depending on which viewport is active. See more details in Chapter 3.

8. **Animation and Time Controls:**

It contains the main controls for animation. These controls are explained in detail in Chapter 2.

9. **Time Slider:**

It allows you to move through any frame of the animation. The Time Slider is explained in detail in Chapter 2.

10. **Status Bar:**

On the left side, there is a two-line interface, where you can create scripts and execute commands. On its right, there is the Status line, which displays the number and type of object(s) selected, and below the Status line, there is the Prompt line, giving instructions on what your next step should be. On the right side of the Status line, there is the Coordinate Display area with the X, Y, and Z fields indicating the coordinates of the selected object and allowing you to control its position (see Section 1.5).

11. **Viewports:**

Everything in 3ds Max is located in a three-dimensional world that is viewed through one or more (up to four) viewports. By using multiple viewports, you can have the best possible visualization of objects in a scene. See more details in Sections 1.2 and 1.5.

If you look at the various toolbars, you will notice a double-dotted line at the beginning of each toolbar. If you move the cursor there, it changes appearance to a double-cross, and you can click and drag to reposition the toolbar in the 3ds Max interface (Figure 1.3). Select the Chaos Corona Toolbar, and drag it to dock it at the left side of the 3ds Max interface. Do the same for the V-Ray Toolbar (Figure 1.4).

To hide or unhide a toolbar, right-click on the double-dotted line at the beginning of a toolbar or on an empty area at any toolbar's ribbon and select/deselect from the pop-up menu any toolbar. Click on the Viewport Layout Tabs and the Scene Explorer – Default to hide them (Figures 1.5 and 1.6).

Figure 1.3

Cursor conversion to a double-cross.

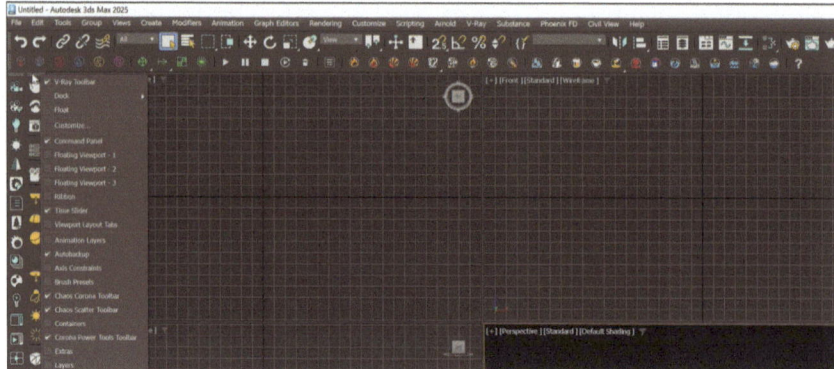

Figure 1.4

The Chaos Corona and the V-Ray Toolbars repositioned on the left side of the interface.

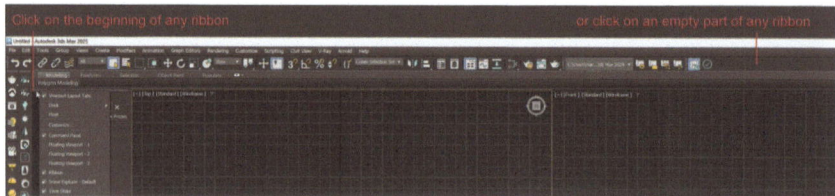

Figure 1.5

Ways to hide/unhide a toolbar.

1.2 Viewports

When you open Autodesk 3ds Max 2025, there are by default four viewports displayed – Top, Front, Left, and Perspective. The multiple viewports help to observe different aspects of the scene. One of the viewports is marked with a highlighted border and is the active viewport, as seen in Figure 1.2. To make a viewport active, simply click in it. Press Alt+W to maximize the active viewport or to switch from one viewport back to the four viewports. Another way to perform this action is to click on the Maximize Viewport Toggle from the Viewport Navigation Controls at the bottom right corner of the 3ds Max interface (Figure 1.7).

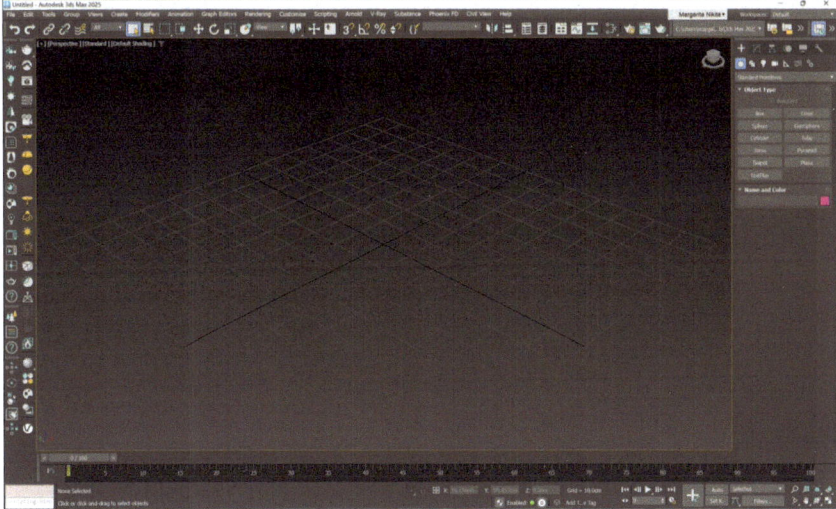

Figure 1.6

Autodesk 3ds Max 2025 interface after the adjustments.

Figure 1.7

Viewport Navigation Controls – Maximize Viewport Toggle command.

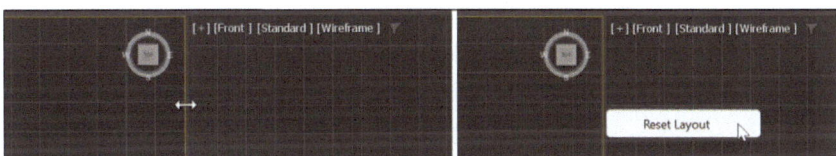

Figure 1.8

Controlling the size of the layout from the intersection of the viewports.

To resize the viewports, drag the intersection of two or four viewports. To return to the original layout, right-click on an intersection and choose Reset Layout (Figure 1.8).

A viewport can be rotated: activate the viewport you want to rotate, hold down the Alt key, hold down the middle mouse button, and drag the mouse. Otherwise, use the Orbit command from the Navigation Controls (Figure 1.9). Note that this command rotates the viewport, and therefore, it rotates all objects in the scene that exist in that viewport. The other viewports remain still. If you want to rotate a specific object in a scene, you should use the Select and Rotate command described in Section 1.5. In this case, the object rotates in all viewports.

To change the number of viewports and their layout, go to the menu Views and choose Viewports Configuration…. Otherwise, in any viewport, click on the General viewport label, [+], and choose Configure Viewports from the pop-up menu. Click on the Layout tab, and choose a layout. Assign what each viewport will display by clicking on the viewport representation and choosing from the pop-up menu. Click OK for the changes to apply (Figure 1.10).

Revert to the default viewport layout. In the lower left corner of each viewport, a three-color world-space tripod is visible. The colors correspond to the three axes of world space: red for X, green for Y, and blue for Z. In the upper right corner of each viewport is the ViewCube. This tool shows the orientation of the scene based on the North direction of the model. Each viewport contains a series of four menus in the top left corner that control the viewport display. The menus are displayed with brackets, and from left to right, they are General, Point-of-View (POV), Shading, and Per View Preference (Figure 1.11).

- **General [+]:** Use this menu to control the viewport display and configuration. Some useful commands are the Maximize Viewport (Alt+W) to maximize/minimize the selected viewport and the Active Viewport command to choose which viewport will become active. Two other useful commands in the General menu are the Show Grids (G) and the Configure Viewports… Use the Show Grids to hide or unhide the viewport grid, and use the Configure Viewports to choose a different layout for the viewports via the Layout tab. The Show Grids command can also be executed by pressing the G key.
- **Point-of-View (POV):** Use this menu to change the active point-of-view; i.e., the position from which we see the scene. Thus, some basic options are Top, Front, Left, Perspective, and Cameras. The Cameras option will be enabled after you place a camera in the scene (see Chapter 3).

Figure 1.9

Viewport Navigation Controls – Orbit command.

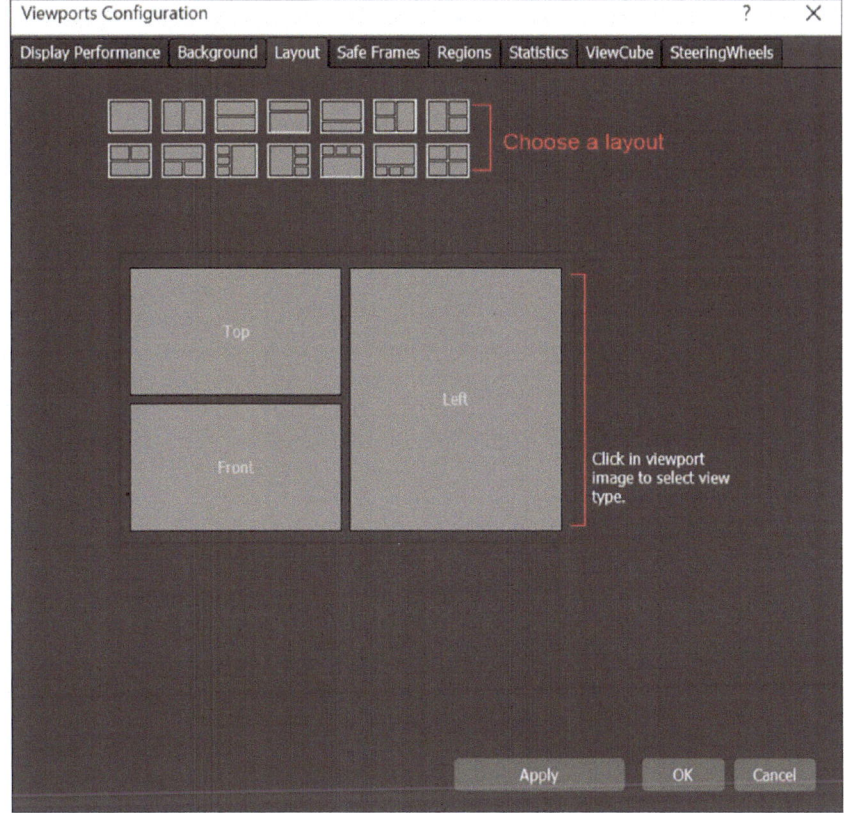

Figure 1.10

Viewports Configuration.

- **Shading:** Use this menu to set the shading of the viewport. The default option is Standard, which applies standard-quality settings for shading and lighting. If, for instance, you choose Performance, the scene will be displayed with a medium gray color. This means that any textures applied will no longer be visible in the viewport, but they will render with the texture. This option can be used in scenes with many polygons to improve the performance of the viewport.
- **Per View Preference:** This last menu controls the way an object is displayed in the viewports. Two are the basic options: Wireframe (or Wireframe Override) and Default Shading. Wireframe Override means that the objects will be displayed as wired objects, while Default shading means that the objects will be displayed with their colors and textures. Another useful option is the Edged Faces. In simple terms, this

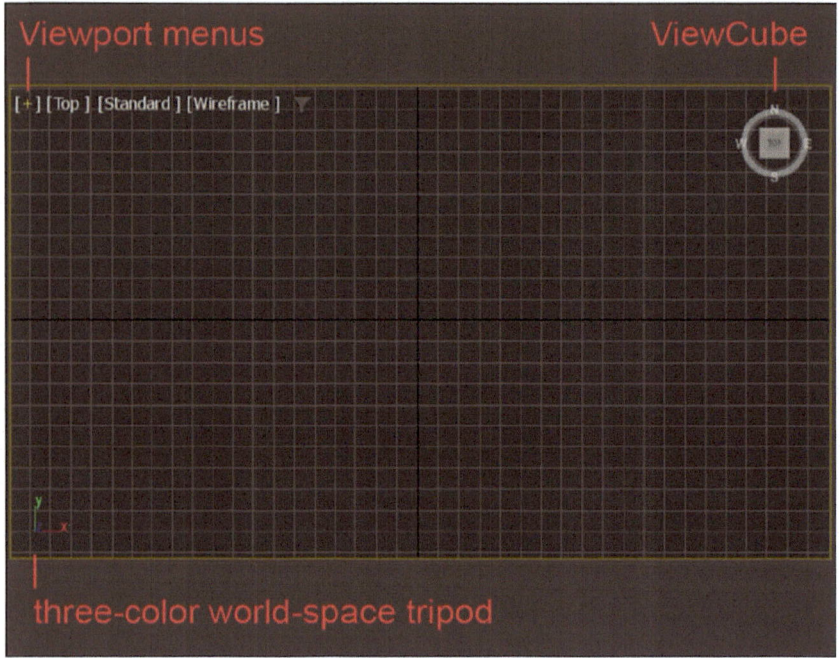

Figure 1.11

Viewport menus, ViewCube, and the three-color world-space tripod.

is a combination of Wireframe and Default Shading. The objects are displayed with the color/texture, whereas the edges are also highlighted when the objects are selected.

As an example, Figure 1.12 shows a box in two Perspective viewports using Wireframe (left) and Default Shading (right) display.

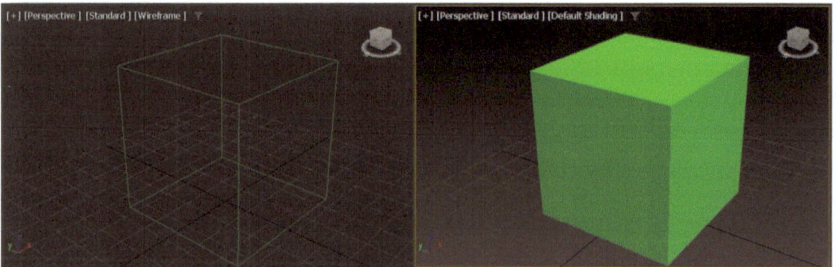

Figure 1.12

Perspective viewports displaying the box in two different ways – Wireframe (left) and Default Shading (right).

1.3 Create and Modify Standard Primitives

In this section, you will create some basic primitives and edit them. You will start with a Box and continue with a Sphere. You should keep in mind that when you do modeling in 3ds Max, the first thing you need to do is to set up the units. Therefore, go to the menu Customize and choose Units Setup. Choose a unit system, for example, Metric, and from the drop-down list, choose the unit scale, say Centimeters. It is also important to click on the System Unit Setup button and set the same units; otherwise, you will not be able to measure correctly (Figure 1.13).

Go to the Command Panel, click on the first tab, Create, and below there is a row of categories you can create. You can choose between Geometry, Shapes, Lights, Cameras, Helpers, Space Warps, and Systems. To create a standard primitive, click on the first button, Geometry. From the drop-down menu, make sure Standard Primitives is selected and click on the Box from the Object Type rollout. Go to the Top viewport, click anywhere, hold down, and drag to create a rectangle, which is the base of the box. Release the cursor to complete the base, then move the mouse to give height to the box, and click to complete the design process (Figure 1.14).

Be careful to set the units from the very beginning when you start the project and not after you have created the geometry of the project.

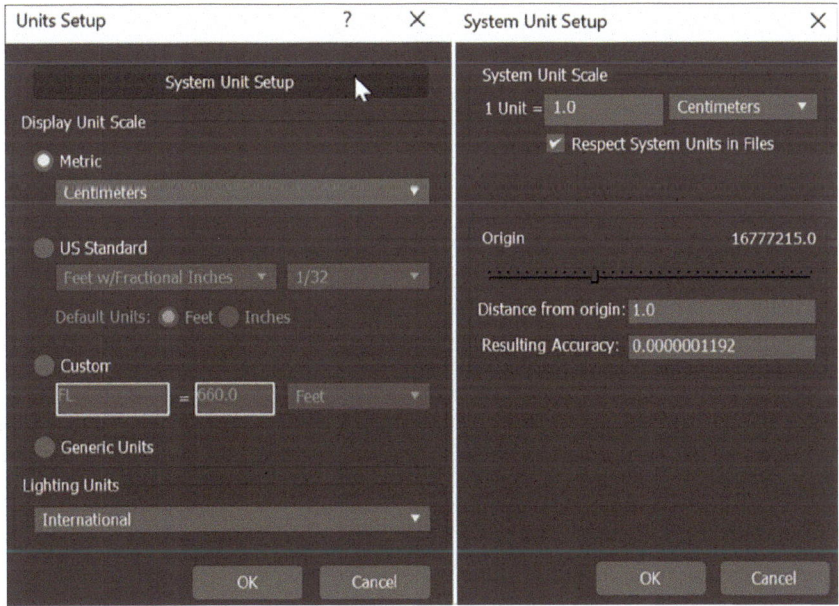

Figure 1.13

System Unit Setup.

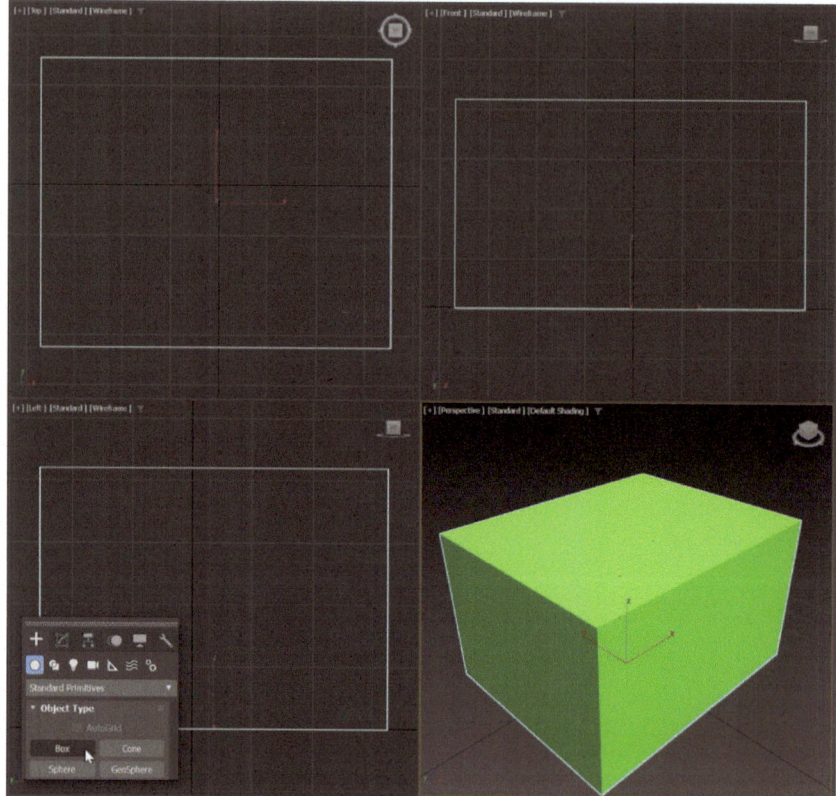

Figure 1.14

Box creation.

When you created the box, you did not specify its dimensions. To do so, with the box selected, go to the Modify tab, the second button in the Command panel. If you want the box to be 50 cm on each side, go to the Length, Width, and Height fields, and type 50 (Figure 1.15).

To see the dimensions of an object in the Modify tab, the object must be selected.

Go to the Navigation Controls at the bottom right corner of the work environment, and click on the Zoom Extends All Selected command. This command zooms in or out the selected object in the viewports (Figure 1.16).

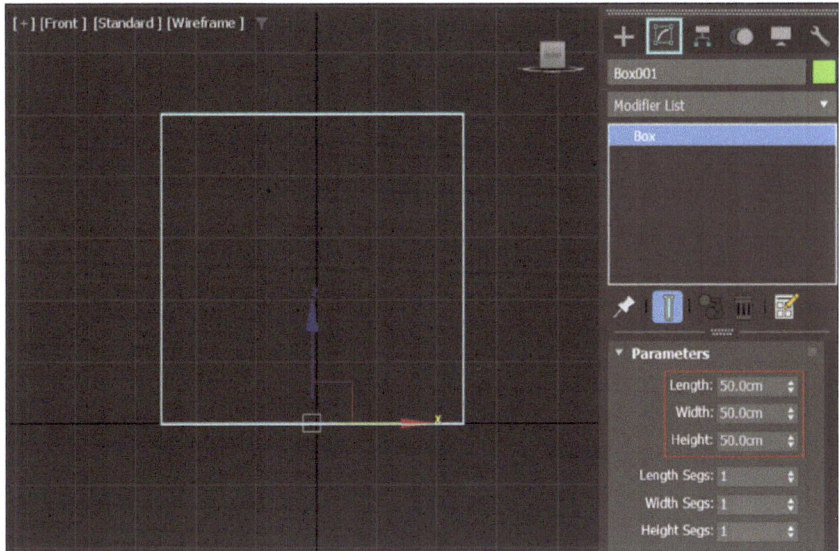

Figure 1.15

Size adjustment of the Box from the Modify tab.

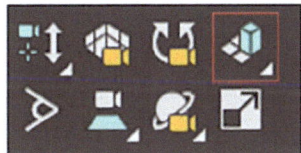

Figure 1.16

Viewport Navigation Controls – Zoom Extends All Selected command.

Create another standard primitive, a Sphere. Go to the Top viewport, and zoom out by scrolling down the middle mouse button to create some space for the sphere. By holding down the middle mouse button, the Pan command is enabled. Move the viewport so that the box is moved to the right. Go to the Create tab, and choose Sphere. In the Top viewport, click and drag to define the radius. When you release the mouse, the sphere is created (Figure 1.17).

As before, the sphere does not have a specific radius. Go to the Modify tab, and type 25 in the Radius field. If you click on the Zoom Extends All Selected command, the sphere will get centered in all viewports. If you want both the box and the sphere to get centered, then click and hold down the Zoom Extends All Selected command and choose Zoom Extends All. Now, all the objects fit in the viewports and not only the selected ones (Figure 1.18).

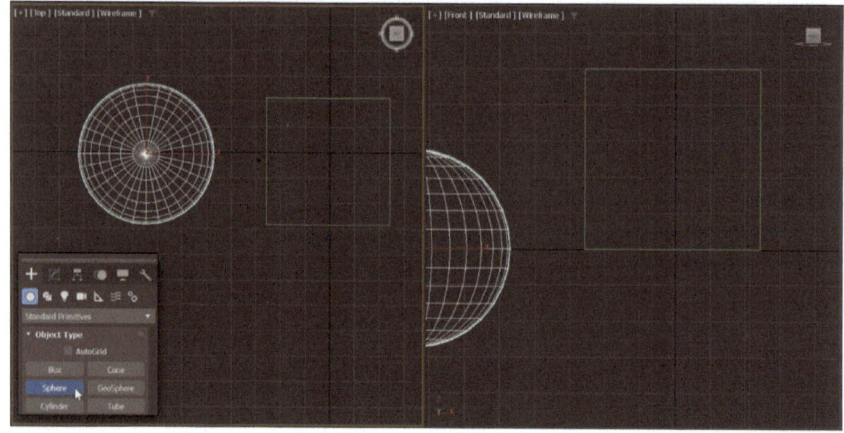

Figure 1.17

Sphere creation.

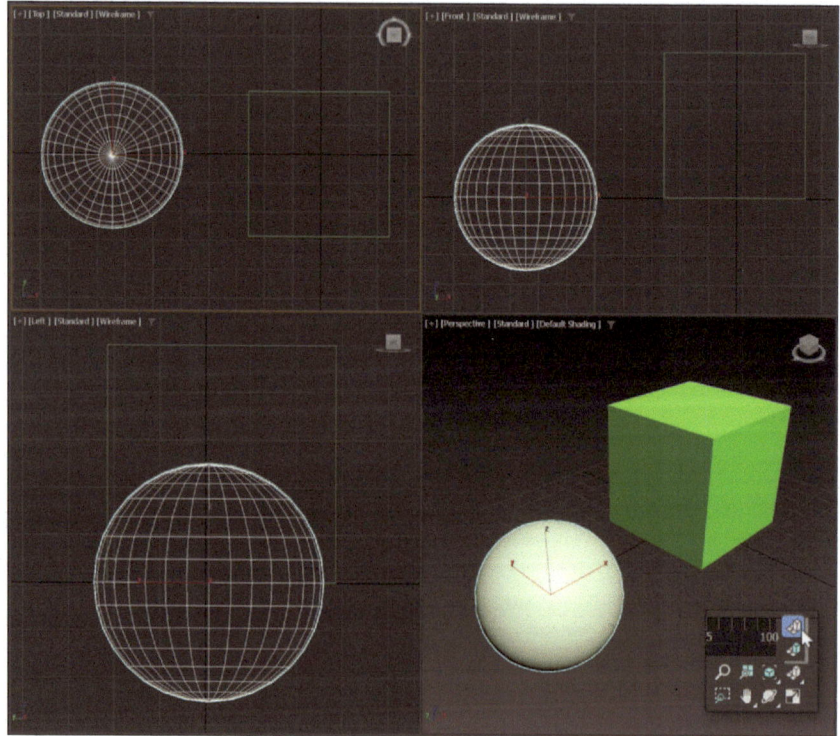

Figure 1.18

Centering all objects in the viewports using the Zoom Extends All command.

1.4 Selecting Objects

To select an object, click on the Select an Object command from the Main Toolbar and then click on the object you want to select (Figure 1.19). If you want to select more than one object, hold down the Ctrl key.

Another way is to click on the Select by Name command. The Select From Scene dialog box appears that shows all the objects of the scene in alphabetical order. If you click on Box001 and press OK, the box is selected (Figure 1.20).

To open the Select From Scene dialog box, you can also press the H key. At the top of the dialog box, you see the same icons that exist in the Create tab in the Command Panel. In the Select From Scene dialog box, they are used to narrow down the research. This is a helpful feature, because in the final scene, you may have hundreds of objects, many cameras, and several lights, so when you narrow down the research by category, it is easier to find what you are looking for. When the icon has a blue background, this category is enabled, and its elements are visible in the list.

When an object is selected, its edges acquire a white color, so that you can easily identify it from the other objects in the scene. Also, an x, y, z coordination system appears on it.

When you create something in 3ds Max, it is automatically named by the software. To see the name, select the object and check the Name and Color field in

Figure 1.19

Part of the Main Toolbar – Select an Object command.

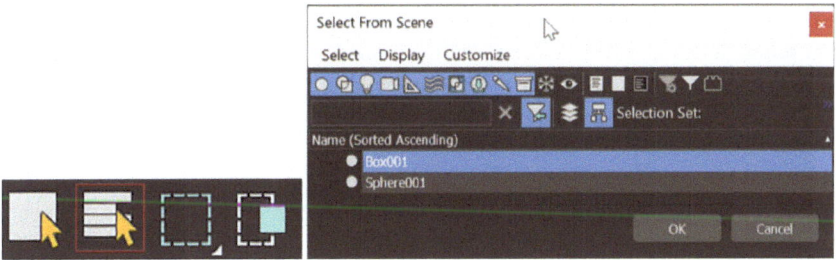

Figure 1.20

Select by Name command (left) and Select From Scene dialog box (right).

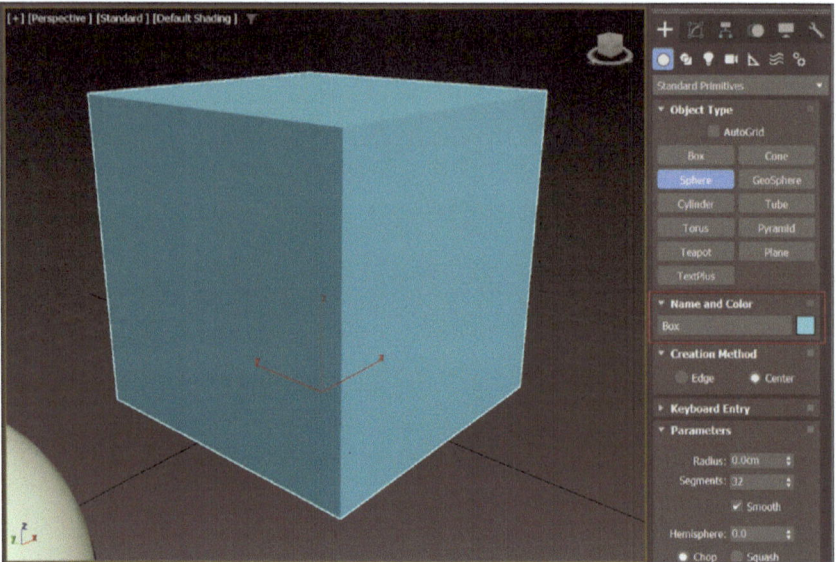

Figure 1.21

Name and Color field.

the Command Panel. To rename it, type in the desired name. Next to the name field is a color swatch. This color is not the material of the object, but the 2D color representation of the object. If you click on the color field and choose a cyan color, the box will become cyan in the Perspective viewport, while in the other viewports, the edges of the box will appear cyan (Figure 1.21).

Go to the Top viewport, and select the box. If you click in another viewport, for example in the Perspective, the viewport activates, but the object gets deselected. To activate a viewport without losing the selection, you must right-click in the new viewport.

1.5 Transform Commands

The transform commands are Select and Move, Select and Rotate, Select and Scale, and Select and Place. Although this book only covers animation techniques and not modeling, these commands are crucial to prepare a scene for animation, and this is the reason we present them.

1.5.1 Select and Move

As its name denotes, use this command to select and move objects. To activate the command, go to the Main Toolbar and click on the Select and Move button or press W (Figure 1.22).

When you activate the Select and Move command, an x, y, z coordination system is placed on the selected object. Depending on the arrow you click on and

Figure 1.22

Part of the Main Toolbar – Select and Move command.

drag, the movement is constrained to the respective axis. If, for instance, you click on the red arrow, which represents the X axis, and drag the cursor, the object moves only along the x axis. Apart from the red, green, and blue arrows, there are also some small planes that connect the axes at the origin. The edges of those planes normally have the color of the axis they touch on. These planes are used to move an object along two axes simultaneously (Figure 1.23).

To move an object by a specific distance, use the Coordinates Display in the Status Bar. If, for instance, you want to move the box 50 cm to the right, enable the Select and Move command, select the box, and go to the X field. These fields show the coordinates of the box. If you click on the Absolute Mode Transform Type-In button, in front of the X, Y, and Z fields, the fields change to zero. Type 50 in the X field, press Enter, and the box moves to the right by 50 cm. Once you press Enter, the value changes again to 0. The name and appearance of the Absolute Mode Transform Type-In button changed to Offset Mode Transform Type-In (Figure 1.24). Click on it to return to the default display of the coordinates of the selected object.

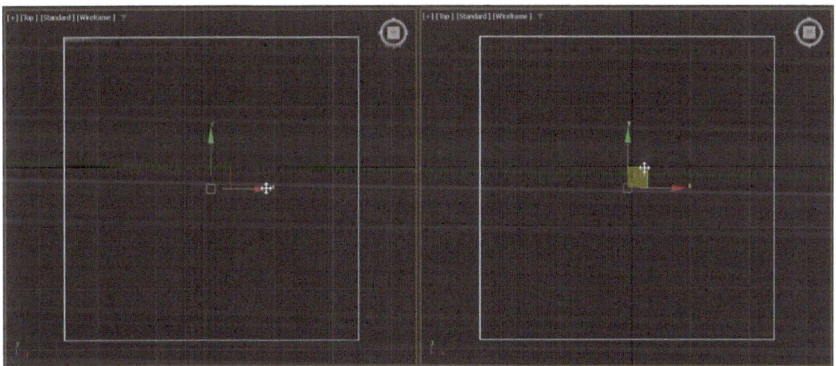

Figure 1.23

Box movement using the arrows (left) or the small plane (right).

Figure 1.24

Absolute Mode (left) and Offset Mode (right) Transform Type-In.

1.5.2 Select and Rotate

To rotate an object, use the Select and Rotate command from the Main Toolbar or press the E key (Figure 1.25).

When this command is enabled, in the Perspective viewport you see three colored circles and an external white one on the selected object, which define the rotation axis. In the other viewports (Top, Bottom, Left, Right, etc.), the three colored circles, due to the projection, are reduced to one colored circle and to a colored cross.

If you click on a circle and drag the cursor up or down, you rotate the object along that circle. Use the Transform Type-In fields to set a specific orbit of the selected object. If, for instance, you type 45 in the Z field, the box will rotate 45° clockwise around the z axis (Figure 1.26).

Figure 1.25

Part of the Main Toolbar – Select and Rotate command.

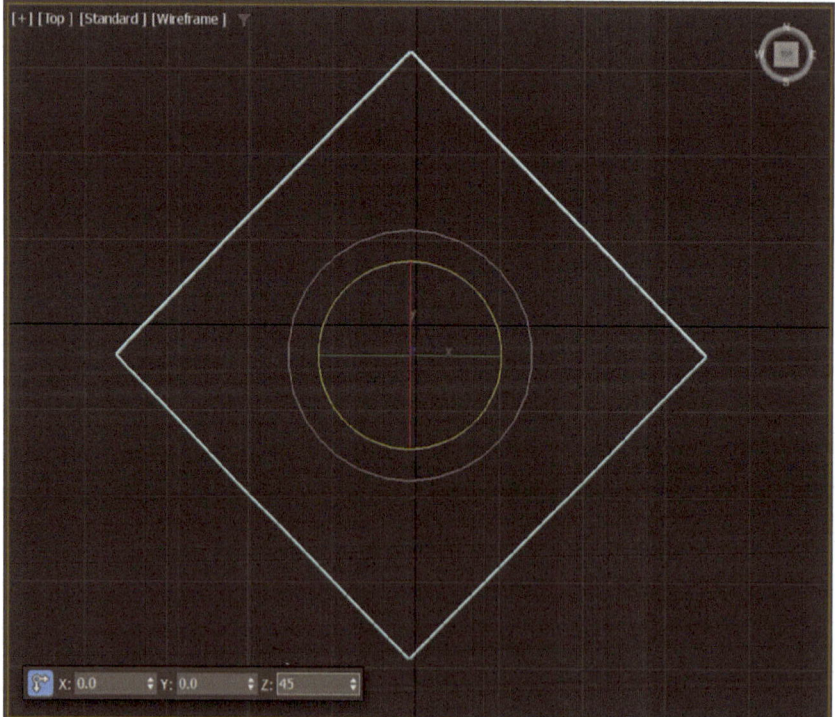

Figure 1.26

Rotating the Box by 45° using the Z Transform Type-In in the Top viewport.

1.5.3 Select and Scale

To scale an object, use the Select and Scale command from the Main Toolbar (Figure 1.27).

As an example, go to the Top viewport, enable the Select and Scale command, and choose the box. Click on the red arrow, and drag to scale the box along the x axis, while if you click on the green arrow and drag, you scale it along the y axis. Apart from the two axes, there are also two triangles that connect the two axes, a highlighted yellow and an outlined yellow. Click and drag on the highlighted yellow to scale the box along the x, y, and z axes simultaneously. If you click and drag on the outlined yellow, then you scale the box along the x and y axes simultaneously, but the z axis remains the same (Figure 1.28).

To scale the selected object by a specific percentage, for example 50%, use the Absolute Mode Transform Type-In fields. With the Top viewport active, go to the X field, type 50, and press Enter. The box becomes half the size.

It is useful to check the Perspective viewport while transforming an object to fully understand the changes you are making.

A point that needs special attention regarding the Scale command is the following. In the previous example, the dimensions of the box were scaled down by 50%.

Figure 1.27

Part of the Main Toolbar – Select and Scale command.

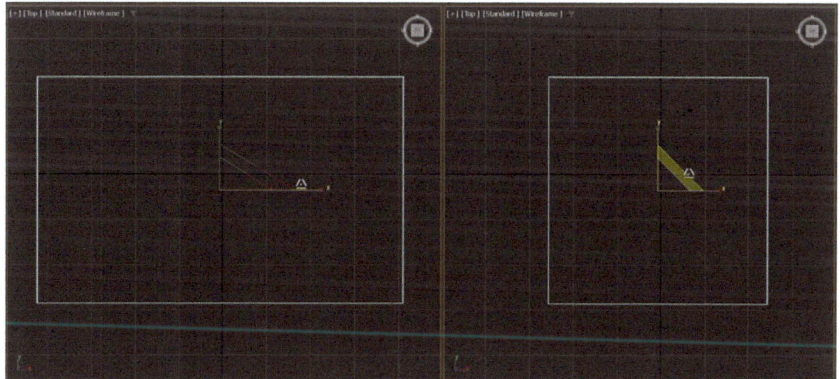

Figure 1.28

Scaling the Box using the arrows (left) or the triangles (right).

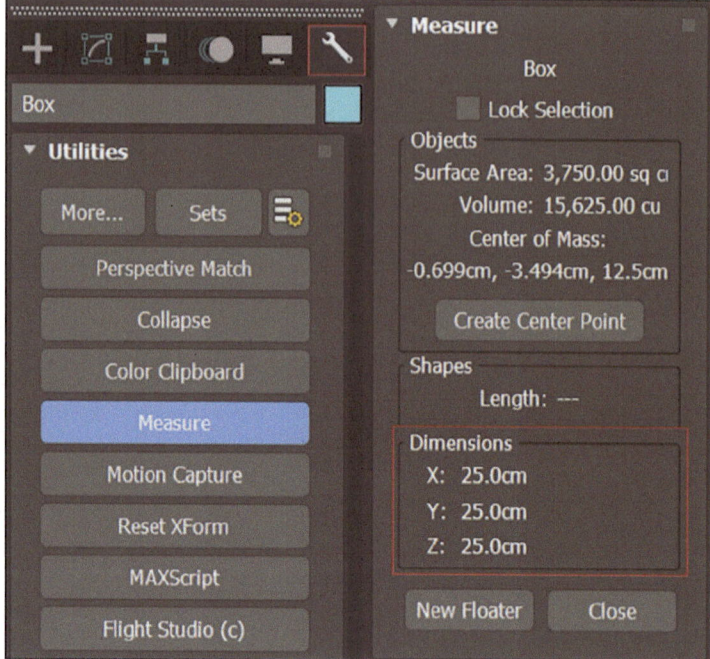

Figure 1.29

Measure command showing the dimensions of the selected object.

Figure 1.30

Part of the Main Toolbar – Select and Place command.

However, if you go to the Modify tab, to check the dimensions of this box, you will notice that they are still 50 cm, while they should be 25 cm. Unfortunately, these fields are not updated when using the Select and Scale command. For this reason, when you want to check the dimensions of a selected object, it is preferable not to use the Modify tab, but the Utilities tab in the Command Panel. More specifically, select the box, go to the Command Panel, and from the Utilities tab, click on Measure. Go to the Dimensions section to see the box dimensions (Figure 1.29).

1.5.4 Select and Place

Use the Select and Place command to position an object accurately on the surface of another object (Figure 1.30). More specifically, go to the Perspective viewport, enable the Select and Place command from the Main Toolbar, select the Box, and move it on the Sphere. The bottom part of the Box aligns with the perimeter of the Sphere (Figure 1.31).

Figure 1.31

Placing the Box on top of the Sphere using the Select and Place command.

1.6 Saving a Project

When you start working on a new project, it is automatically named Untitled by the software. To rename it, you need to save it. To save a project, go to the menu File and choose Save or press CTRL+S. In the Save File As dialog box, type in the desired name, and choose the destination folder. If you press CTRL+S again, the Save File As dialog box does not appear since you have already named the project, and you just save the progress of the file.

I strongly advise you to keep saving a project often while you are working on it, especially when you work with heavy files, with many polygons, so that you will not have any unpleasant surprises; for instance, 3ds Max may crash, and you may lose your progress.

1.6.1 Save As

The Save As command allows you to save a project under a different name, in a different location, or in a different version. For example, go to the menu File and choose Save As or press SHIFT+CTRL+S. The Save File As dialog box appears. From the Save type as field, you can choose the 2021 version. In this way, you can share your file with users who have an earlier version of 3ds Max.

3ds Max allows you to save to formats up to three versions prior to the current version.

1.6.2 Save Selected

The Save Selected command allows you to save in a separate file only the selected object(s). If, for instance, you click on the box and go File > Save Selected, rename it to box, and press Save, the box is saved in a new 3ds Max file.

1.6.3 Archive

Archive is an important command, which allows you to move a file from one computer to another or exchange files. 3ds Max works with paths. When you load a texture to apply it as a material or an .ies file, 3ds Max recognizes the path you follow to load these external files. If you change the location of any of these files or the location of the project, then your project will no longer render properly. Archive creates a compressed archive file that contains the scene file and any other files referenced by it, i.e., textures, ies, XRef, and so on.

To understand this option, open the file Chapter 3.max. Go to the menu File, and choose Archive. The File Archive dialog box appears in which you define the destination folder. Give it a few minutes, and a Dos screen will appear (Figure 1.32). Once it disappears, the archive is created. Go to the destination folder you saved it. If you open it, you see the .max file along with folders that contain the maps used in this project.

> To share a project, first you need to archive it and then share the zip file. If you only send the .max file, then all the textures and external files will be missing.

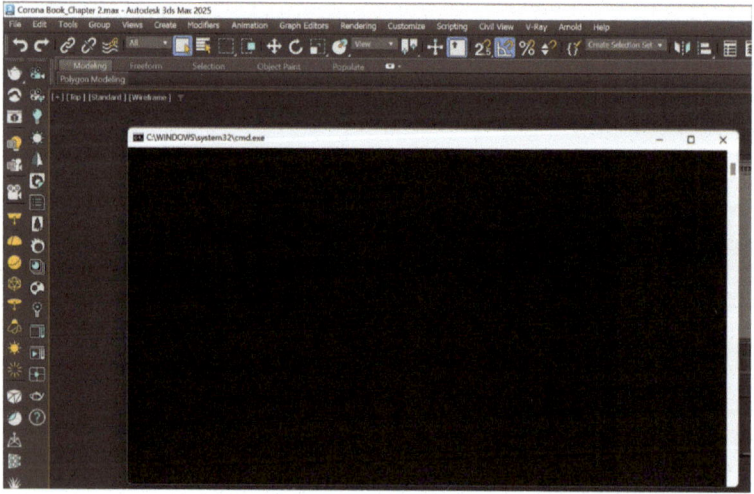

Figure 1.32

The Dos screen when archiving a project.

2

Animation Basics in 3ds Max

2.1 Introduction to Animation Controls

Before creating your first animation in 3ds Max, it is essential to understand two foundational tools: the Time Slider and the Animation Controls. These tools are the backbone of the animation process, and understanding them will ensure a smooth workflow.

2.1.1 The Time Slider and Track Bar

The Time Slider and Track Bar (Figure 2.1) are located on the Status Bar. These tools can be docked or floated, offering flexibility in arranging your workspace for optimal efficiency. Key components include the following:

A. **Back up Time One Unit:**
   It moves the Time Slider back by one unit, whether that is a frame or a specific time increment, depending on your settings. This is ideal for reviewing your animation step by step.

B. **Time Slider:**
   It allows you to move quickly between frames. Drag it to scrub through your animation, and see how your scene looks at different points in time. It is a handy way to preview your work frame by frame.

DOI: 10.1201/9781003651222-2

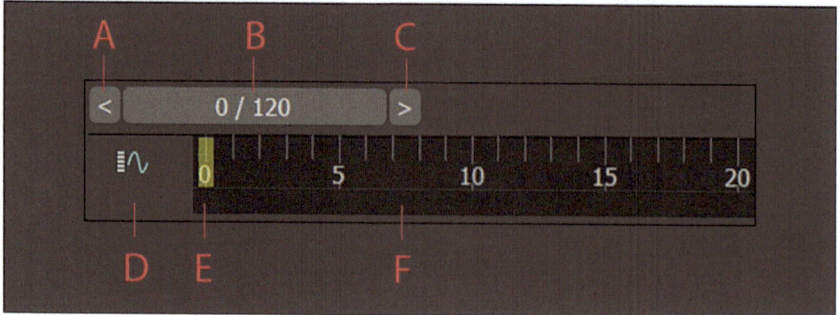

Figure 2.1

The Time Slider and Track Bar.

C. **Forward Time One Unit:**
   It moves the Time Slider forward by one unit, whether that is a frame or a specific time increment, depending on your settings.

D. **Open Mini Curve Editor:**
   It opens the Mini Curve Editor directly within the interface. The Curve Editor lets you adjust animation curves for smooth transitions and fine-tune the movement of your objects. It is a quick way to edit timing and motion without leaving the main workspace.

E. **Current Frame Indicator:**
   It shows the exact frame number or time the Time Slider is currently on. It is a helpful way to keep track of your position in the Timeline.

F. **Timeline:**
   It is a horizontal bar that shows the full range of frames in your animation. It provides a visual reference for where your Time Slider is positioned and allows you to easily scrub through your animation or select specific frames to work on.

2.1.2 The Animation Controls

Located at the bottom of the interface (Figure 2.2), between the Status Bar and the Viewport Navigation controls, the Animation Controls allow you to play back and manage animations directly in the viewports. Key features include the following:

A. **Go to Start (Home):**
   It moves the Time Slider to the first frame of the active animation, so you can quickly start from the beginning.

B. **Previous Frame:**
   It moves the Time Slider one frame backward.

C. **Play/Stop Animation:**
   This button starts or stops your animation in the active viewport.

Figure 2.2

Main Animation Controls and Time controls for animation playback within viewports.

Click Play to watch the animation, and while it is playing, the button changes to Stop, and so you can pause it anytime.

D. Next Frame:

It moves the Time Slider forward by one frame.

E. Go to End (End):

It moves the Time Slider to the last frame of the active animation, letting you jump straight to the end.

F. Key Mode Toggle:

It allows you to quickly move between the keyframes in your animation. By default, it works with the keyframes shown in the timeline below the Time Slider.

G. Current Frame (Go To Frame):

It displays the current frame number or time where the Time Slider is positioned. You can also type in a specific frame number or time to jump directly to that point in your animation.

H. Time Configuration:

Clicking this button opens the Time Configuration window, where you can adjust important animation settings like Frame Rate, Time Display, Playback options, and overall Animation Length.

I. Set Keys:

It allows you to manually create keyframes for the selected object. Use it to save specific changes, like position, rotation, or scale, exactly when and where you want them in your animation Timeline. It works together with the Key Filters to give you precise control over what gets keyframed.

J. Auto Key Mode Toggle:

When this is turned on, any changes you make to an object's position, rotation, or scale are automatically saved as keyframes in your animation. This makes it easy to record movements as you go.

K. **Set Key Mode Toggle:**

This mode allows you to manually create keyframes for selected objects and specific tracks, such as position, rotation, or scale. Unlike Auto Key, it gives you full control over what changes to keyframe and when, using the Set Keys button and Key Filters.

L. **Default In/Out Tangents for New Keys:**

This flyout lets you choose a default tangent type for new animation keyframes. Tangents control how movement transitions between keyframes, affecting the smoothness or sharpness of the motion. You can set this for keys created using either Set Key Mode or Auto Key Mode.

M. **Selection List:**

It shows all the objects you currently have selected in your scene. It helps you keep track of which objects you are working on and allows you to quickly switch between them for editing and animation.

N. **Key Filters:**

Let you control which types of changes (like position, rotation, scale, or others) are recorded when creating keyframes. You can customize these filters to focus only on the aspects of your animation you want to adjust, giving you precise control over the keyframing process.

2.2 Animation Settings

In this section, you will dive into the Animation Settings, which can be accessed through the Time Configuration window. To open it, simply click on the Time Configuration button, . Once inside, you will notice these settings are grouped into four main sections: Frame Rate, Time Display, Playback, and Animation (Figure 2.3).

2.2.1 What Is a Frame?

Before diving into the settings, it is crucial to understand what a frame is. In animation, a frame represents a single rendered image. When frames are played in sequence, they create the illusion of motion.

The smoothness of an animation is measured in frames per second (fps) – the number of frames displayed every second. Standard animations typically run at 24–30 fps, depending on the desired level of fluidity and project requirements.

For example, at 30 fps, one second of animation requires 30 individual frames, meaning 30 rendered images are needed to produce a single second of motion.

2.2.2 Frame Rate

The Frame Rate section defines the playback speed of your animation in frames per second (fps). You can choose from the following options:

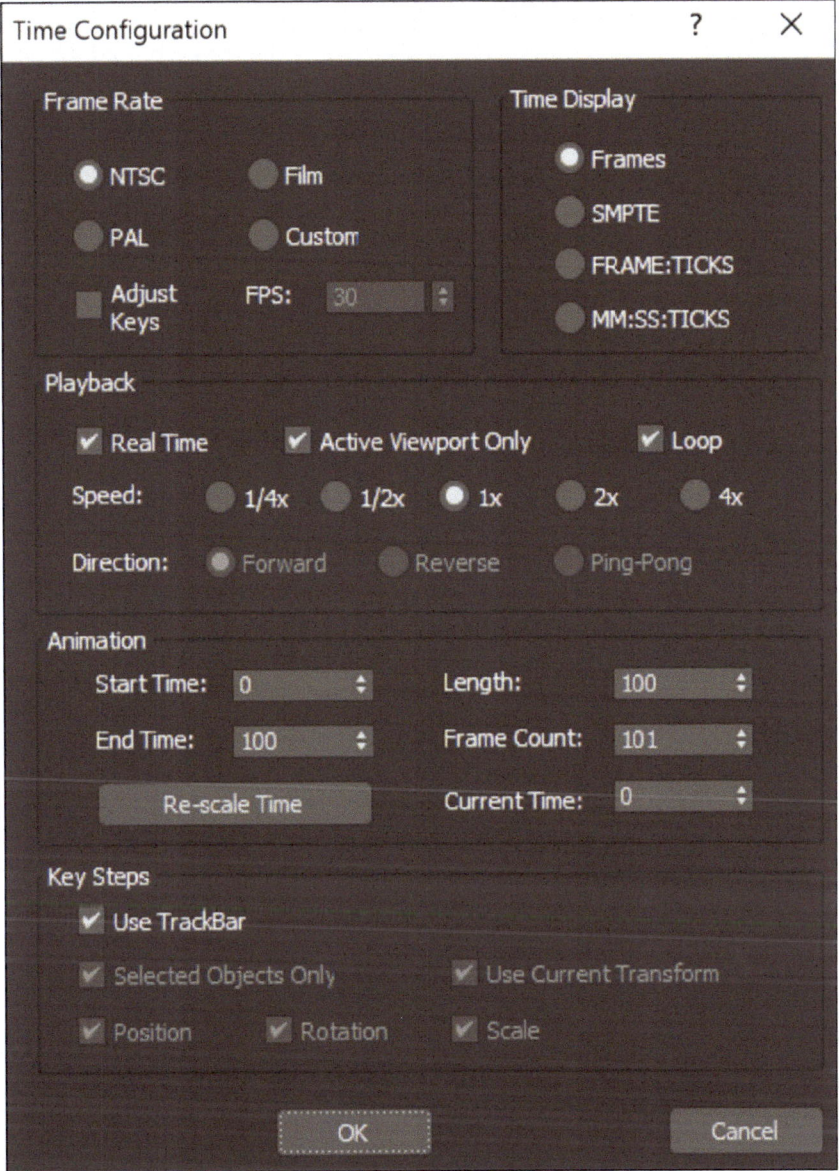

Figure 2.3

The Time Configuration dialog.

- **NTSC (30 fps):**
  This stands for National Television System Committee and is the standard frame rate used in North America, Canada, and Japan for television and video. While it is commonly referred to as 30 frames per

second, the actual frame rate is slightly more precise at 29.97 fps. This minor difference ensures compatibility with broadcast standards in these regions.

- **PAL (25 fps):**
  This stands for Phase Alternating Line and is the standard frame rate for television in most of Europe, parts of Asia, and Australia. This setting uses 25 fps and is widely used in regions where PAL is the broadcasting standard.

- **Film (24 fps):**
  This is the traditional frame rate used for movies and cinematic productions. It runs at 24 fps, providing the smooth, natural motion associated with classic film and digital cinema.

- **Custom:**
  This allows you to specify a custom frame rate tailored to your specific project needs by entering the desired value in the FPS field. This is ideal for animations that require non-standard frame rates.

Each frame rate is optimized for the technology and viewing preferences of its region or medium. Selecting the correct frame rate is essential and depends on where your animation will be displayed, as it affects playback smoothness and compatibility with the intended platform (TV, film, or online).

For most architectural animations, 30 fps is a versatile and reliable choice. It balances cinematic quality with smooth motion, is perfect for online and digital platforms, and is widely accepted globally. This makes it the safest option for general-purpose animations.

2.2.3 Time Display

The Time Display settings determine how the Timeline is displayed (Figure 2.4). These options control how you view and interact with the timing of your animation. The options include the following:

- **Frames:**
  These display the timeline in simple frame numbers, making it easy to track the position of each frame. For example, if your animation runs at 30 fps, Frame 90 corresponds to 3 seconds. This is the most commonly used option for animators.

- **SMPTE:**
  This stands for the Society of Motion Picture and Television Engineers format. It displays time as Hours:Minutes:Seconds:Frames (e.g., 00:00:03:15). This format is ideal for projects that need to match specific timecodes, such as video or broadcast productions.

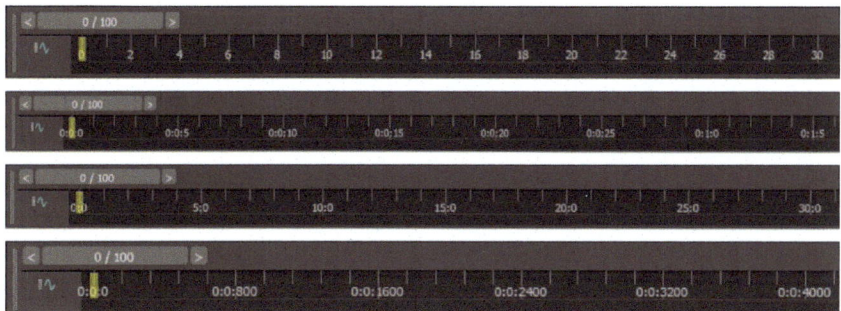

Figure 2.4

The Timeline adjusted depending on the Time Display option selected. From top to bottom: Frames, SMPTE, Frames:Ticks, and MM:SS:Ticks.

- **Frame:Ticks:**
  This displays the timeline as a combination of frames and ticks, where ticks are sub-frame units for finer control. For example, 90:4,800 indicates Frame 90 with 4,800 Ticks. This is useful for precise adjustments in complex animations.
- **MM:SS:Ticks:**
  This shows time in Minutes:Seconds:Ticks (e.g., 01:30:2,400). Ticks represent subdivisions of a second, allowing detailed timing adjustments. This format is helpful for syncing animations to audio or other timed elements.

Each option serves a specific purpose, so choose the one that best fits your project's needs and workflow. For most workflows, the default Frames setting is ideal.

2.2.4 Playback

The Playback settings allow you to control how your animation plays back within the viewports. These options ensure that the playback speed and behavior suit your needs during the animation process. The following is a breakdown of the options:

- **Real-Time:**
  This ensures that the animation plays back at the selected frame rate (i.e., 24 fps, 30 fps). If your system cannot keep up with real-time playback due to a heavy scene, frames might be skipped to maintain timing. Use this option to preview your animation as it would appear when rendered.
- **Active Viewport Only:**
  This plays the animation in the currently active viewport instead of all viewports. This reduces processing load, which can be helpful for improving playback performance in complex scenes.

- **Loop:**
  When checked, the animation restarts from the beginning after reaching the last frame. This is ideal for testing continuous or cyclic animations, such as walking loops or rotating objects.
- **Speed:**
  This option allows you to adjust the speed of the animation from a quarter of the normal speed to four times faster.
- **Direction:**
  This controls the playback direction.
  - Forward: This plays the animation from the first frame to the last frame in a straight sequence.
  - Reverse: This plays the animation backward from the last frame to the first frame. This is useful for testing reverse motion effects.
  - Ping-Pong: This plays the animation forward to the last frame and then reverses back to the first frame in a continuous loop. This is helpful for reviewing seamless transitions in both directions.

Recommendations:

- Use Real-Time for accurate previews.
- Enable Loop for cyclic animations.
- Choose Ping-Pong for back-and-forth movements, like sliding doors.
- Keep the Speed at 1x for realistic timing.

2.2.5 Animation

The Animation section defines the structure and timing of your animation. The following is a detailed explanation of the settings available:

- **Start Time:**
  This defines the frame where your animation begins. For example, setting the Start Time to 0 means your animation will start at Frame 0. You can adjust this to shift the starting point, if needed.
- **End Time:**
  This sets the frame where your animation ends. For example, if your animation runs at 30 fps and you set the End Time to 90, the animation will last for 3 seconds.
- **Length:**
  This shows the total duration of the animation in frames. It is calculated as the difference between the Start Time and the End Time. You can adjust this value directly, and 3ds Max will automatically update the Start and End Times accordingly. For example, if your Start Time is 0 and you set the Length to 90, the End Time becomes 90 and the Timeline automatically contracts (or expands) to reflect the new Length (Figure 2.5).

the object to look at a particular point in the timeline. The animation software interpolates the motion or transformation between keyframes, creating a smooth transition.

For example, if you set a keyframe for a Box at Frame 0 with a position at (0,0,0) and another keyframe at Frame 50 with a position at (10,0,0), the software will calculate the in-between frames, so the Box moves smoothly from (0,0,0) to (10,0,0).

2.3.2 Auto Key vs. Set Key

- **Auto Key:**
  This mode automatically creates a keyframe whenever you make changes to an object's properties during animation. It is faster and more intuitive for simple animations, but requires caution, as it records every change you make.
- **Set Key:**
  This mode gives you precise control. You manually create keyframes by pressing the Set Key button after making changes. It is ideal for complex animations where you want to avoid unintentional keyframes.

2.3.3 Examples

You will begin with a simple animation of a box and a sphere. This will help you get familiar with using keyframes and the Timeline before you start applying these concepts to more complex scenes.

2.3.4 Step-by-Step Example: Animating a Box with Auto Key

Step 1. Creating a Box.
1. **Create the Box:**
   - Go to the Command Panel, select the Create tab, and choose Box.
   - In the Top Viewport, click, hold, and drag to create the base of the Box. Then, drag your cursor upward to add height, and click again to complete the Box.
2. **Set dimensions:**
   With the Box selected, navigate to the Modify tab and set its dimensions to 10 cm x 10 cm x 10 cm.
3. **Position the Box:**
   Enable the Select & Move command. In the Coordinates Display, set the Box position to (0, 0, 0).
   The Box is now positioned at the origin point (Figure 2.6).

Step 2. Setting Keyframes.
1. **Add the first keyframe:**
   - Select the Box, and ensure the Time Slider is at Frame 0.
   - Click Auto Key to enable it. The Timeline turns red to indicate it is active.
   - A keyframe is automatically added at Frame 0 (Figure 2.7).

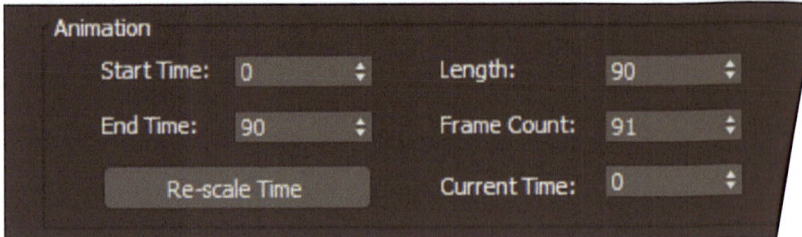

Example of adjusting the Length value. If Length is set to 90 with Start Time c
End Time will become 90.

- **Frame Count:**
  This defines the total number of frames in your animatior
  Length, this value directly correlates with how many frames are
  within the Timeline, regardless of the frame rate.
- **Current Time:**
  This displays the current frame where the Time Slider is
  You can enter a frame number here to jump directly to that ǁ
  timeline.
- **Re-scale Time:**
  This option lets you change the timing of your entire anir
  out altering its structure. For example, if your animation i
  long and you re-scale it to 200 frames, the animation will
  slowly while maintaining all keyframe positions proportio

2.2.6 Examples

- If you want to create a 5-second animation at 30 frames p
  to determine how many frames are needed, you multiply
  seconds) by the frame rate: 5 seconds × 30 fps = 150 fram·
  This means you need to set your Animation Length
  the Time Configuration window.
- If you have 100 frames in your timeline and you want t
  tion of your animation at the same frame rate (30 fp∫
  frames by the frame rate: 100 frames/30 fps = 3.33 secc
  This tells you the animation would last 3.33 sec·
  these settings, you can control the timing and length
  effectively.

2.3 Getting Started with Keyframes

2.3.1 What Is a Keyframe?

A keyframe is a marker in time that stores specific values
ties, such as position, rotation, or scale. Think of it as a sna

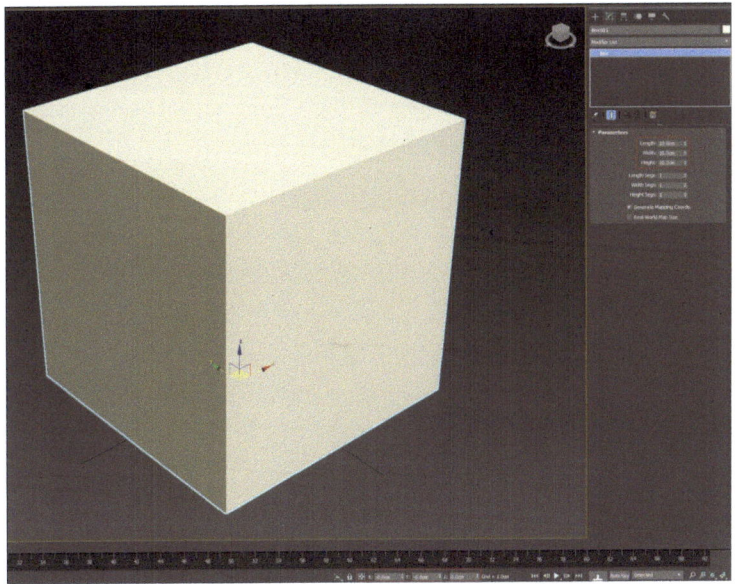

Figure 2.6

Box with Length, Width, and Height 10cm and positioned at (0,0,0).

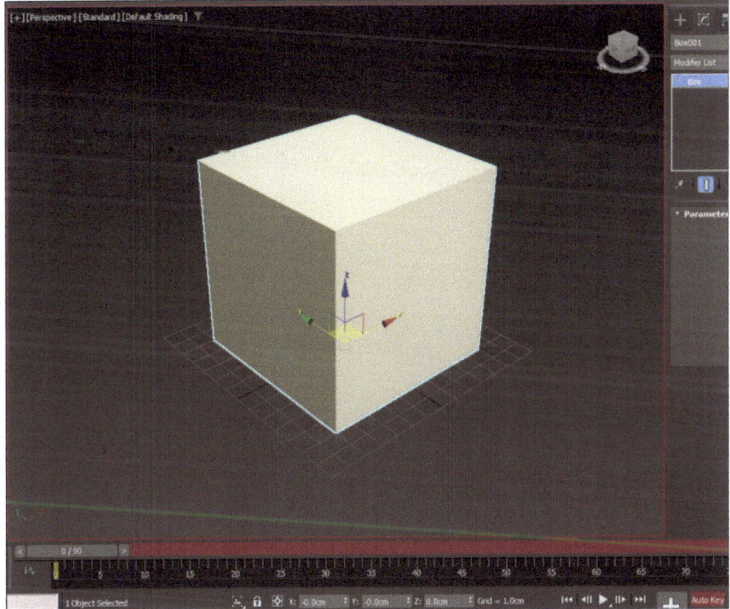

Figure 2.7

Enabling Auto Key mode and adding a keyframe at Frame 0.

2. **Add the second keyframe:**
   - Drag the Time Slider to Frame 100.
   - With the Box selected, and the Select & Move command enabled, enter 10 in the X field in the Coordinates Display to move the Box 10 cm along the X-axis.
   - Another keyframe is added at Frame 100 (Figure 2.8).
   - Click Auto Key again to disable it.

Step 3. Preview the Animation.

Press the Play button to see the Box move from Frame 0 to Frame 100 (Video 2.1).

2.3.5 Step-by-Step Example: Animating a Sphere with Set Key

Step 1. Create the Sphere.
1. Go to the Command Panel, select the Create tab, and choose Sphere.
2. In the Top Viewport, click, hold, and drag to define its diameter.
3. With the sphere selected, navigate to the Modify tab and set the radius to 5 cm.
4. Enable the Select & Move tool. In the Coordinates Display, set the sphere's position to (0, 0, 5).

After positioning the sphere, you will not be able to see it since it is hidden inside the Box (Figure 2.9). If you click and drag the Time Slider ahead of Frame 0, you will be able to partially see the sphere. At Frame 100, the sphere will be fully visible (Figure 2.10).

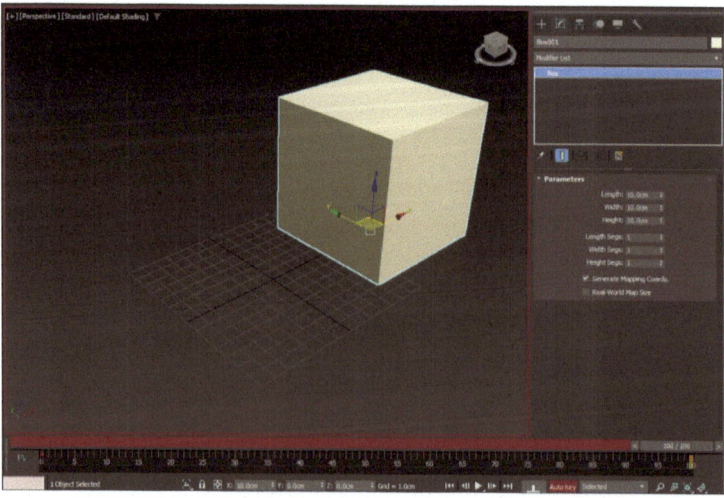

Figure 2.8

Adding a second keyframe to Frame 100 with the Auto Key mode.

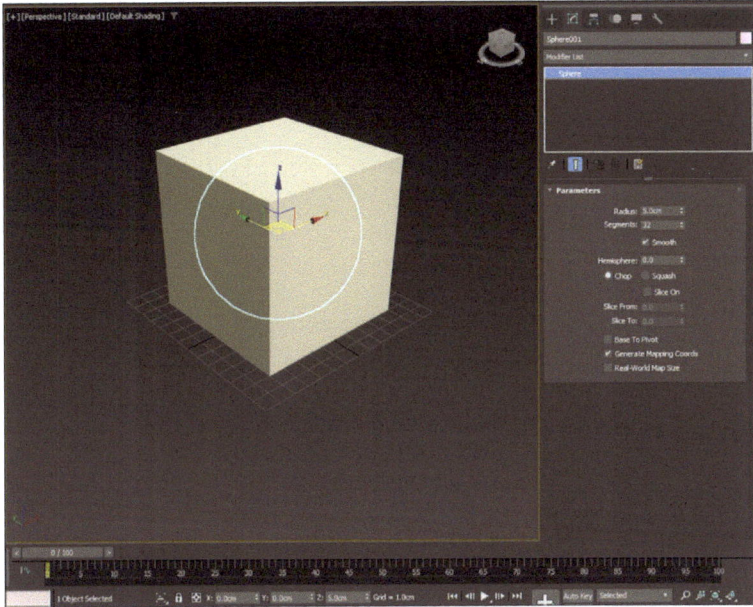

Figure 2.9

Sphere hidden inside the Box at Frame 0.

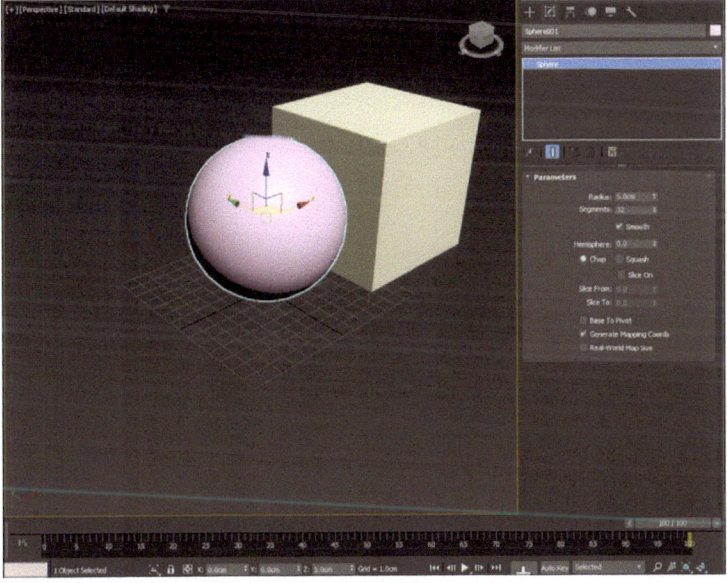

Figure 2.10

Sphere fully visible at Frame 100.

Step 2. Add the First Keyframe.

1. Select the sphere and ensure the Time Slider is at Frame 0.
2. Click Set Key to enable it. The Timeline will turn red to indicate it is active.
3. Press the Set Keys button, 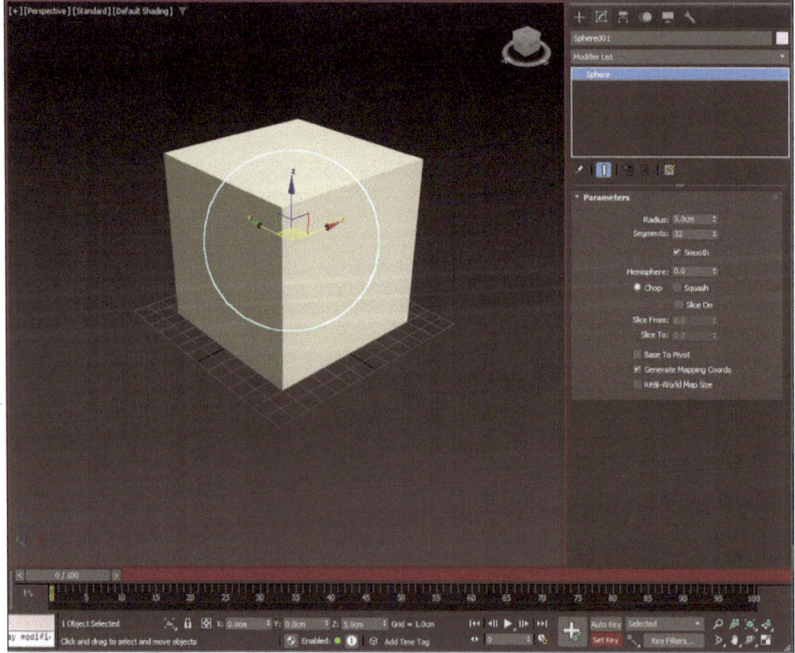, to add a keyframe (Figure 2.11).

Step 3. Add the Second Keyframe.

1. Drag the Time Slider to Frame 100.
2. With the sphere selected, enter 10 in the Y field to move the sphere 10 cm along the Y-axis.
3. Press the Set Keys button to add the Final Keyframe (Figure 2.12).
4. Click Set Key again to disable it.

Step 4. Preview the Animation.

Press the Play button, and you will watch both the sphere and the Box moving (Video 2.2). The sphere smoothly moves from its starting position (Frame 0) to 10 cm along the Y-axis (Frame 100), while the Box to 10 cm along the X-axis (Frame 100).

This method provides precise control over keyframe placement and is perfect for ensuring your animations are deliberate and organized.

Figure 2.11

Activating the Set Key mode with the Sphere selected and adding a keyframe at Frame 0 using the Set Keys button.

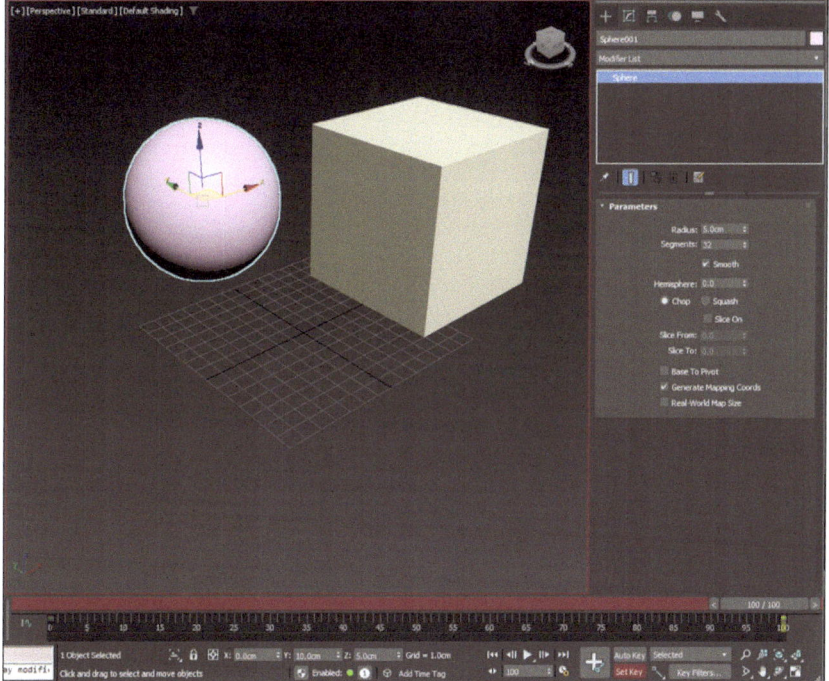

Figure 2.12

Moving the sphere 10 cm along the Y-axis and clicking the Set Keys button to add a keyframe at Frame 100.

2.3.6 Adjusting Keyframes for Timing

One important feature to keep in mind is that you can move keyframes directly on the Timeline to adjust the timing of your animation.

For instance, if you wanted the animation of the Box to be twice as fast, you could select the last keyframe, currently at Frame 100, and drag it to Frame 50 (Figure 2.13). By doing this, the Box will have fewer frames to complete the assigned path, resulting in a shorter animation duration.

You can immediately notice this change when you press the Play button: the Box will move along the path at a faster pace, and from Frame 50 to Frame 100, it remains still (Video 2.3). This simple adjustment allows you to fine-tune the timing of your animations without having to recreate or modify keyframes manually.

2.3.7 Copying Keyframes for Repeated Motion

You can also copy keyframes on the Timeline. To create looping motion:

1. Select the Box, and then select the first keyframe on the Timeline (Frame 0).
2. Hold Shift, and drag the keyframe to the last frame, Frame 100.

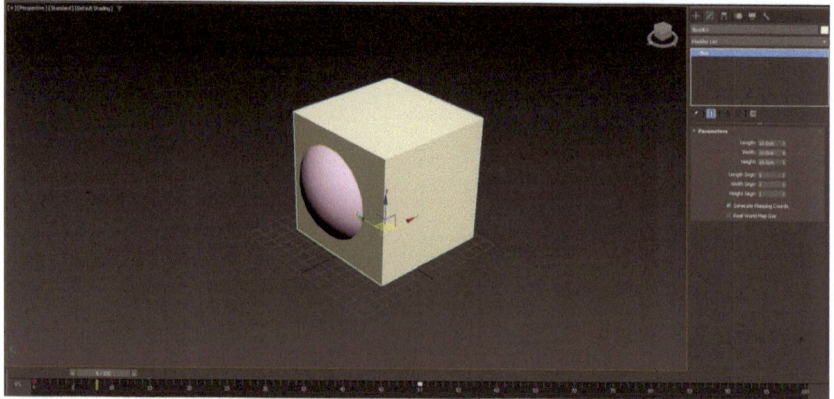

Figure 2.13

With the Box selected, moving the keyframe from Frame 100 to Frame 50.

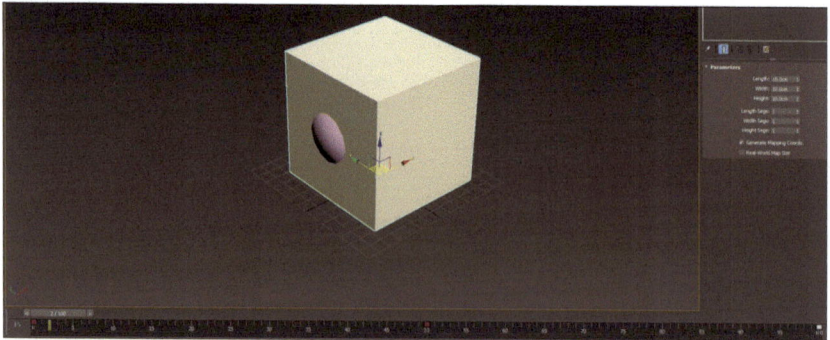

Figure 2.14

Copying the keyframe at Frame 0 to Frame 100 using the Shift key and dragging it.

By doing so, the keyframe is copied without losing its original information (Figure 2.14). Since this keyframe was created when the Box was at (0,0,0) at Frame 0, the copied keyframe at Frame 100 will return the Box to the same position.

When you press Play, you will notice that the Box moves from (0,0,0) to (0,0,10) at Frame 50 and then back to (0,0,0) at Frame 100, creating a smooth back-and-forth motion (Video 2.4).

This technique is incredibly useful for creating repeating animations or symmetrical motion patterns, saving time and effort in recreating keyframes manually.

2.3.8 Deleting Keyframes from the Timeline

When working with animations in 3ds Max, you might need to delete specific keyframes or all keyframes on the timeline.

Create Stunning Animations Using Corona and V-Ray in 3ds Max

To delete a specific keyframe:

1. Select the Object.
2. Navigate to the Timeline to locate the keyframe, and click on it. The selected keyframe will highlight/change color to indicate it is active.
3. Press the Delete key on your keyboard to remove the selected keyframe. Alternatively, right-click on the keyframe, and choose Delete Selected Keys from the context menu (Figure 2.15).

To delete all keyframes:

1. Click and drag to create a rectangle selection around all the keyframes in the Timeline.
2. Once all keyframes are highlighted, press the Delete key on your keyboard.

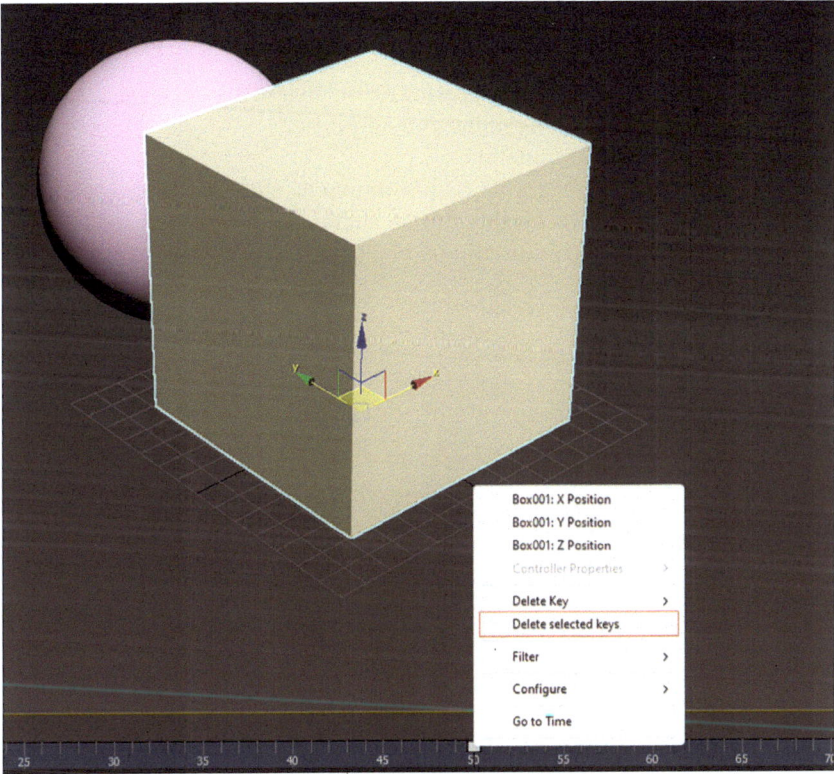

Figure 2.15

Deleting the Box's keyframe at Frame 50 using the right-click.

Once deleted, the animation will no longer include the motion or transformation information stored in that keyframe. For example, if you delete the middle keyframe of the Box's animation at Frame 50, the Box will immediately jump from Frame 0 to Frame 100 without any smooth transition. This practically means that the Box will stay stationary throughout the animation because its position at both Frame 0 and Frame 100 is the same, (0,0,0).

2.4 Animating Parameters

In 3ds Max, animation is not limited to the position, rotation, or scale of objects – you can also animate their parameters. This flexibility opens limitless possibilities for creative motion. The following are a few examples to illustrate this concept.

2.4.1 Step-by-Step Example: Animating the Height of the Box

Step 1. Enable Auto Key.
1. Select the Box, and click Auto Key.
2. Drag the Time Slider to the end of the Timeline (Frame 100).

Step 2. Adjust the Height.
1. In the Modify Panel, reduce the Box's Height to 1cm.
2. Notice a red bracket appearing on the Height parameter (Figure 2.16), indicating that this value is now animated.

Step 3. Preview the Animation.
Press Play to see the smooth, continuous motion. The Box alternates between its original height of 10 cm at Frame 0 and the reduced height of 1 cm at Frame 100 as the animation plays (Video 2.5).

Figure 2.16

A red bracket appears on the Height parameter of the Box indicating that this parameter is being animated.

2.4.2 Step-by-Step Example: Animating the Hemisphere Value of a Sphere

Next, you will animate the Hemisphere parameter of a sphere, demonstrating how object properties can dynamically change over time.

Step 1. Enable Auto Key.
1. Select the Sphere.
2. Turn on Auto Key so that any changes you make will be recorded as keyframes.

Step 2. Animate the Hemisphere Value.
1. Drag the Time Slider to Frame 100.
2. In the Modify Panel, set the sphere's Hemisphere value to 1.
3. A red bracket appears next to the Hemisphere parameter, indicating that this value is now animated. Moreover, the Sphere disappears at Hemisphere value 1 (Figure 2.17).
4. Disable the Auto Key.

Step 3. Preview the Animation.
Press Play to see the animation. The sphere will gradually disappear from the viewport (Video 2.6).

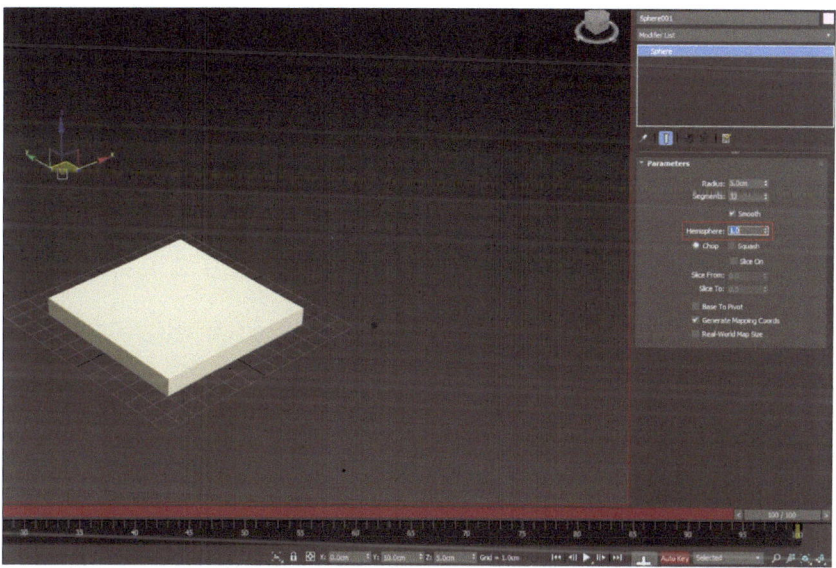

Figure 2.17

A red bracket appears on the Hemisphere parameter of the Sphere indicating that this parameter is being animated. The Sphere at Hemisphere value 1 disappears from the viewport.

2.5 Animating Modifiers

In 3ds Max, animation is not limited to transforming objects; you can also animate Modifiers, adding another layer of dynamic motion to your scenes. By animating Modifiers, you can transform basic shapes into visually engaging forms. You will explore this concept by animating the Bend and Skew modifiers using the Box and Sphere from earlier examples.

2.5.1 Step-by-Step Example: Animating the Bend Modifier

Step 1. Prepare the Box.
1. Select the Box, and increase its segments for smoother bending.
2. In the Modify Panel, set the Length Segs, Width Segs, and Height Segs to 30 (Figure 2.18).

Step 2. Add the Bend Modifier.
From the Modifier List, select Bend.

Step 3. Animate the Modifier.
1. Turn on Auto Key.
2. Drag the Time Slider to Frame 100, and set the Bend Angle to −105 and the Bend Axis to Y.
3. A red bracket appears next to the Angle parameter (Figure 2.19).
4. Disable Auto Key.

Step 4. Preview the Animation.
Press Play to see the Box gradually bending (Video 2.7).

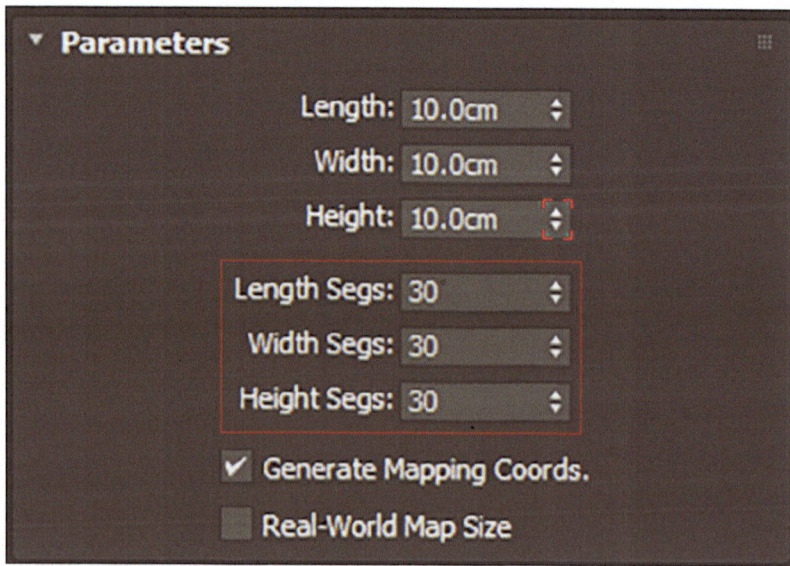

Figure 2.18

Setting the Box's Segments to 30.

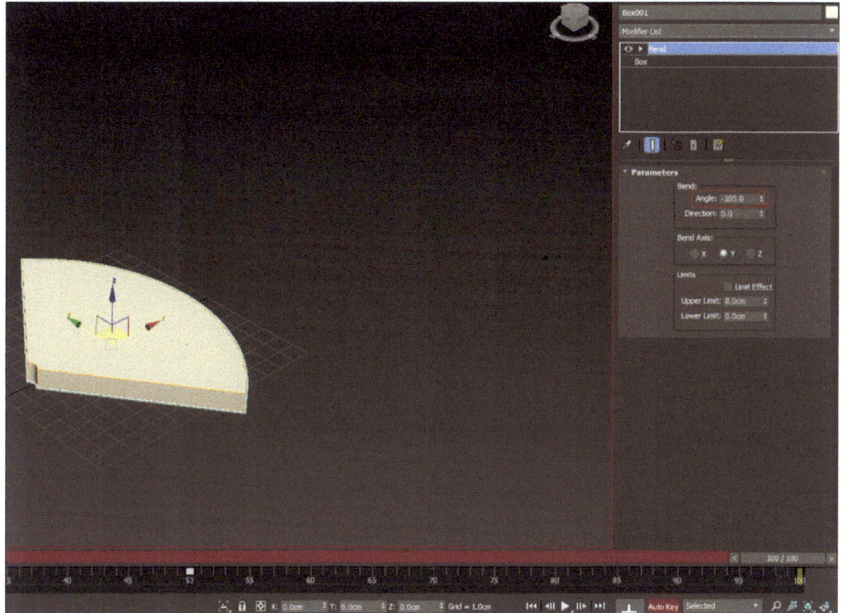

Figure 2.19

Adding the Bend Modifier to the Box. A red bracket appears next to the Bend Angle parameter of the Box indicating that this parameter is being animated.

2.5.2 Step-by-Step Example: Animating the Skew Modifier

Step 1. Prepare the Sphere.
1. Select the Sphere.
2. In the Modify Panel, set the Sphere's Segments to 120 (Figure 2.20).

Step 2. Add the Skew Modifier.
   From the Modifier List, select Skew.

Step 3. Animate the Modifier.
1. Turn on Auto Key.
2. Drag the Time Slider to Frame 50, and set the Skew Amount to 2.5 cm.
3. A red bracket appears next to the Skew Amount parameter (Figure 2.21).
4. Disable the Auto Key.

Step 4. Preview the Animation.
   Press Play to watch the sphere transform dynamically (Video 2.8).

Animating modifiers allows you to transform basic shapes into dynamic, expressive forms. Continue experimenting with different modifiers to push your creativity further.

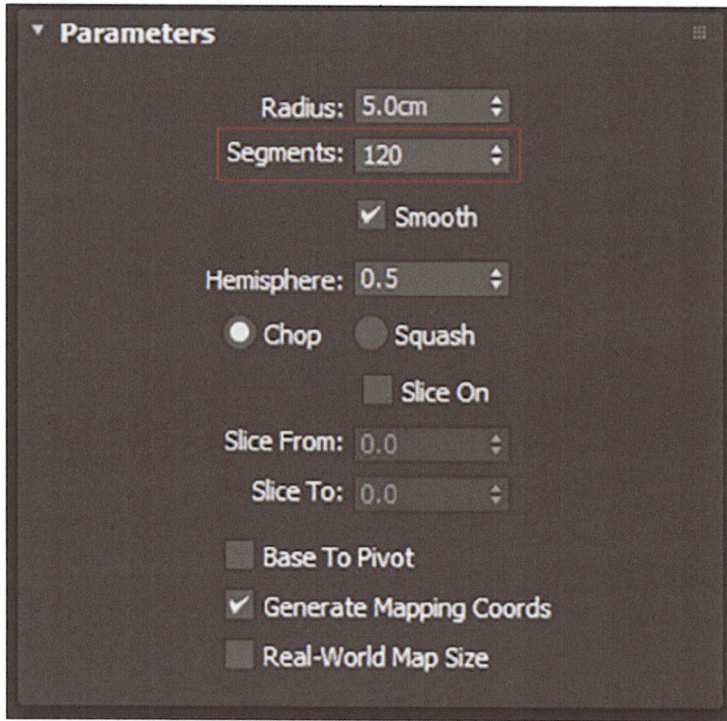

Figure 2.20

Setting the Sphere Segments to 120.

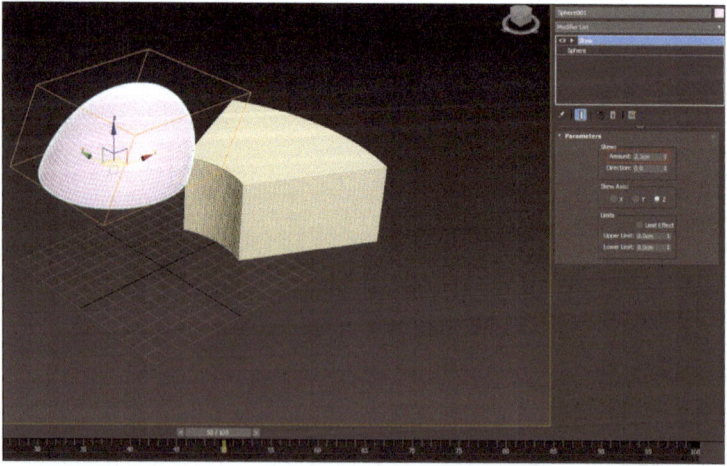

Figure 2.21

Adding the Skew Modifier to the Sphere. A red bracket appears next to the Skew Amount parameter of the Sphere indicating that this parameter is being animated.

2.6 Curves

In animation, Curves are graphical representations of an object's transformations, modifier changes, or any animated properties over time. They allow you to fine-tune the motion, timing, and easing of your animation.

This section explores how to use the Curve Editor in 3ds Max, applying it to the Box and Sphere you created earlier.

2.6.1 Accessing the Curve Editor

To open the Curve Editor, click the Open Mini Curve Editor button, , located on the left side of the Timeline (Figure 2.22).

2.6.2 Overview of the Curve Editor

The Curve Editor interface is divided into the sections illustrated in Figure 2.23:

- **Menus and Main Toolbar:**
  Found at the top, these provide essential tools for manipulating curves and keyframes, such as the Move Keys Tool or Add Keys Tool.
- **Hierarchy Panel (Left):**
  A tree-like structure listing all scene objects and their animatable properties.

Figure 2.22

The Open Mini Curve Editor button on the left side of the Timeline.

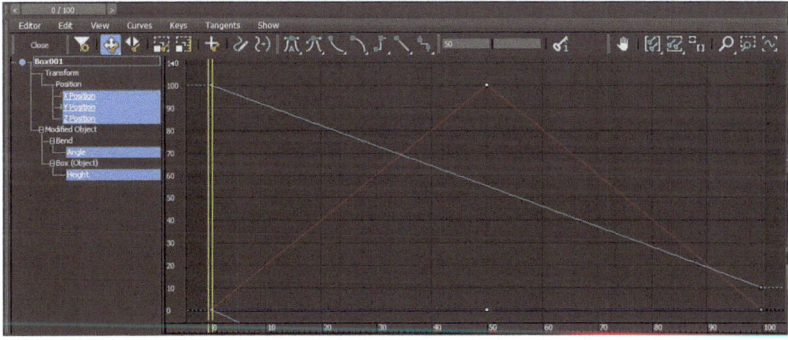

Figure 2.23

The Curve Editor displaying the Box's curves.

- **Curve Display Area (Right):**
    The main graph where curves are displayed. The horizontal axis represents time (in frames), while the vertical axis shows the value of the animated property.

2.6.3 Step-by-Step Example: Adjusting the Box's X-Position Curve

Step 1. Prepare the Box.
  1. Select the Box.
  2. In the Modify Panel, delete the Bend Modifier you added earlier.
Step 2. Select the X-Position Curve.
  1. In the Hierarchy Panel of the Curve Editor, click on the X-Position.
  2. The Curve Display Area will now show only the curve representing the Box's position change over time (Figure 2.24).
Step 3. Adjust the Tangents.
  1. Select the tangent at Frame 50.
  2. Click the Set Tangents to Auto button, ![icon], in the Main Toolbar.
  3. Adjust the tangents, using the Bezier handles to fine-tune the curve shape, as seen in Figure 2.25.
Step 4. Preview the Animation.
    Press Play to see the animation (Video 2.9).

2.6.4 Understanding Ease In and Ease Out

When playing the animation, you will notice the following:

- **From Frame 0 to Frame 50:**
    The Box slows down as it approaches the keyframe, known as Ease In.
- **From Frame 50 to Frame 100:**
    The Box speeds up as it moves away from the keyframe, known as Ease Out.

These easing effects help create natural, smooth motions, ideal for objects slowing to a stop or gradually accelerating.

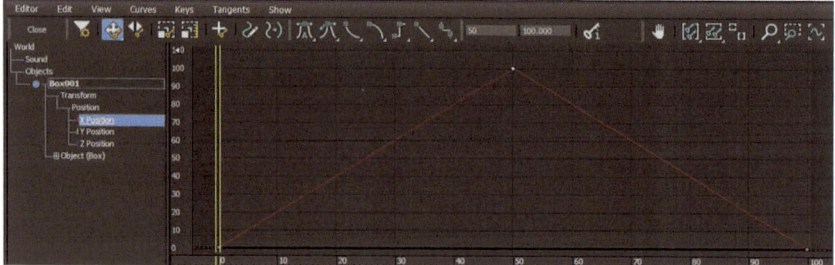

Figure 2.24

The Curve Editor displaying the Box's X-Position Curve.

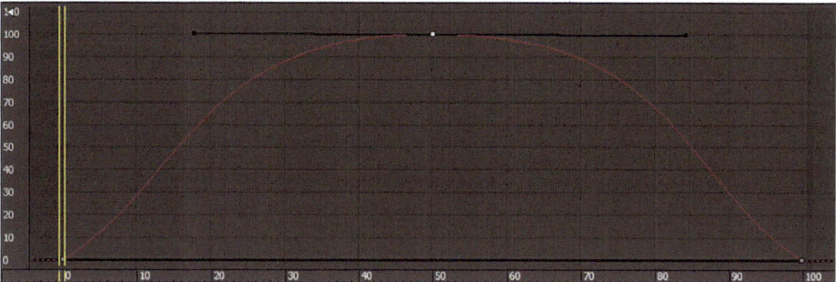

Figure 2.25

The curve after adjusting the tangent at Frame 50.

2.6.5 Choosing the Right Motion

- **Ease In/Ease Out:**

    Perfect for natural, smooth movements, such as a ball rolling to a stop or an object gradually gaining momentum.

- **Linear Motion:**

    Best suited for mechanical or robotic movements, where constant speed is required.

    By understanding and adjusting easing behaviors in the Curve Editor, you can fine-tune your animations to match the desired look and feel, ensuring precision and professionalism in your projects.

3

Camera Animation

3.1 Simple Camera Animation

Animating a camera's position is one of the most fundamental techniques in creating dynamic visualizations. To explore this type of animation, open the file Chapter 3, which is a bedroom interior scene in 3ds Max (Figure 3.1).

3.1.1 Animating the Position of the Camera

The first type of animation to explore is to move the position of the camera. More specifically, to move the camera closer to the bed. To do so, first you need to go to the Time Configuration and set the Frame Rate to 30 fps. Moreover, set the Length to 90 frames (Figure 3.2). This way, the animation will last 3 seconds (90/30 = 3).

3.1.1.1 Step-by-Step Example: Animating the Position of the Camera

Step 1. Select the Camera.
1. Select Camera 01.
2. Enable the Select & Move tool to adjust its position.

DOI: 10.1201/9781003651222-3

[+] [Camera 01] [Standard] [Default Shading]

Figure 3.1

The bedroom interior scene used as an example in this chapter.

Step 2. Animate the Camera.
1. Activate Auto Key to start recording transformations.
2. Drag the Time Slider to Frame 90 on the Timeline.
3. Move the camera forward to the desired position, as illustrated in Figure 3.3 – bottom. Figure 3.3 – top – shows the position of the camera at Frame 0.
4. Disable Auto Key to stop recording changes.

Step 3. Test the Animation.

Play the animation to preview the camera's motion (Video 3.1).

Be mindful that Camera 01 has Camera Clipping enabled. If the camera moves too far forward, the bed will be clipped, resulting in part of it being visually cut off. To avoid this, ensure that the camera stops just before the Near clipping plane intersects the bed. If further forward movement is necessary, adjust the Near value to extend/reduce its range and prevent clipping (see Section 3.2). This adjustment ensures that all desired elements remain visible within the camera view while maintaining smooth animation.

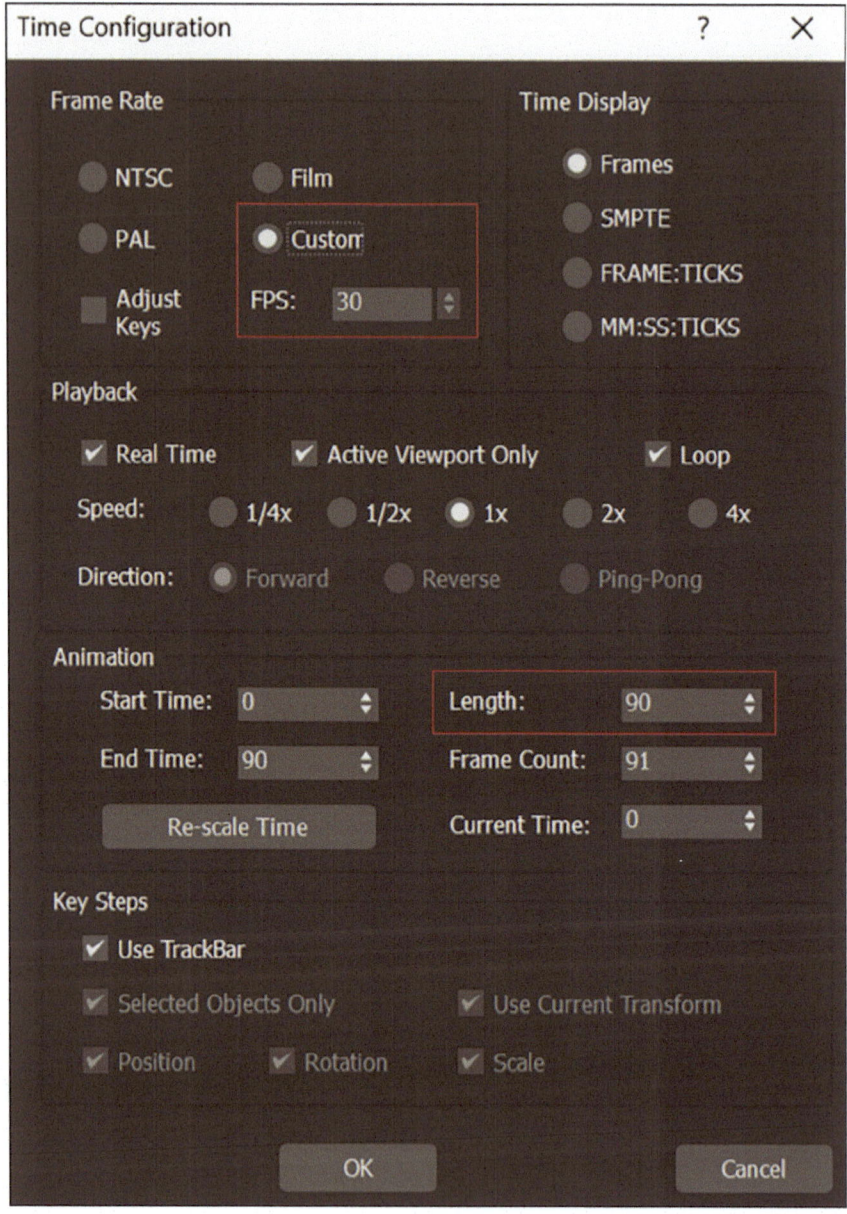

Figure 3.2

Time Configuration with 30 fps and 90 frames Length.

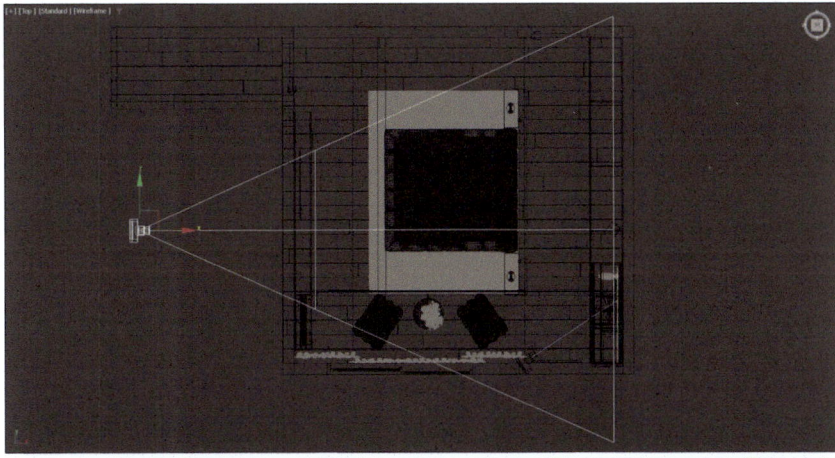

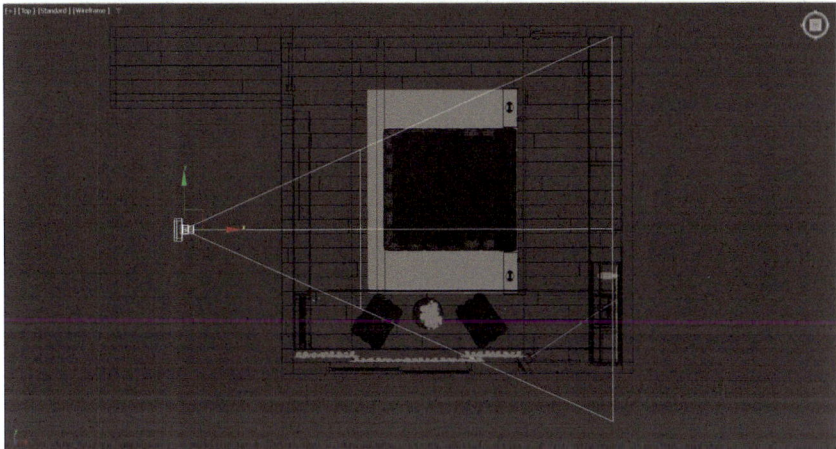

Figure 3.3

Camera position at Frame 0 (top) and camera position at Frame 90 (bottom) in the Top viewport.

3.1.2 Animating the Position of the Camera and the Camera Target

In the next example, the animation involves moving both the camera and its target to create a dynamic motion across the room. For this example, you will move the camera from the left side of the room to the right side, while maintaining focus on the key elements of the scene.

As before, the Timeline is set to 90 frames, giving the animation a total duration of 3 seconds at 30 fps.

Figure 3.4

Camera position at Frame 0 (top) and camera position at Frame 90 (bottom) in the Camera 01 viewport.

If you make larger movements, consider extending the Timeline, i.e., setting more frames in the Length value (i.e., 120, 150, etc.) to avoid creating a disorienting effect for the viewer.

3.1.2.1 Step-by-Step Example: Animating the Position of the Camera and the Target

Step 1. Create a New Camera.

1. Create a new camera either from scratch or by duplicating an existing one in the scene.
2. To duplicate the existing camera:
   - Select both the camera and its target by clicking on the line connecting the two.
   - Enable the Select & Move tool, hold the Shift key, and drag the camera as seen in Figure 3.5.
   - In the Clone Options window, choose Copy.

Be cautious when choosing Instance, as any changes made to the new camera will automatically apply to Camera 01. For this example, it is essential to select Copy instead, as the two cameras will require different settings. By creating a copy, the cameras remain independent, allowing each to have unique configurations without affecting the other.

Step 2. Set the Camera Viewport.

1. Switch the viewport to the new camera:
   - Go to the Camera 01 viewport.
   - Click on the viewport name label, Camera 01, and select Camera 002 from the dropdown menu (Figure 3.6).

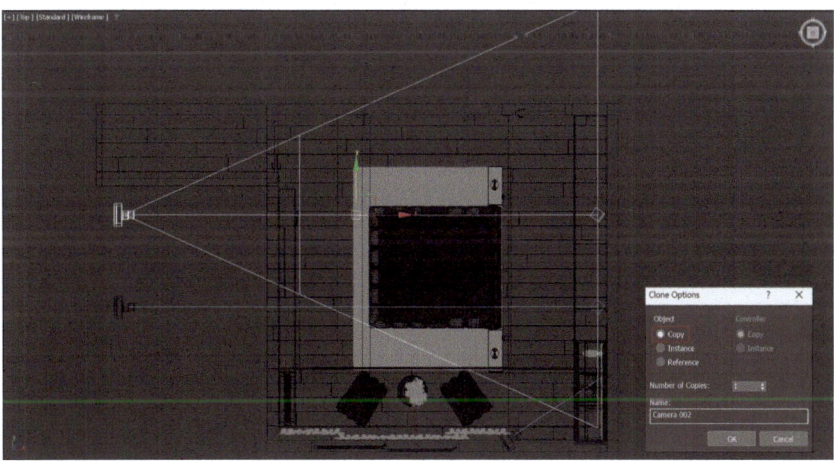

Figure 3.5

Creating a Copy of Camera 01 and positioning it to the left side of the room.

Figure 3.6

Camera002 Viewport at Frame 0.

Step 3. Clear Keyframes from the New Camera.
1. When duplicating a camera, the new camera inherits the original's animation data.
    – Press the Play button, and the copied camera will replicate the original camera's motion, such as slowly moving forward.
2. To remove this animation:
    – Select Camera 002.
    – Navigate to the Timeline, and click and drag to create a selection rectangle around all the keyframes.
    – Press the Delete button to clear the keyframe, making the camera static (Video 3.2).

Step 4. Animate the Camera.
1. Enable Auto Key.
2. Move the Time Slider at Frame 90.
3. Move Camera 002 smoothly to the right side of the room, ensuring it follows a natural horizontal path (Figures 3.7 and 3.8).
4. Disable Auto Key.

Step 5. Test the Animation.
   Play the animation to ensure that the camera moves as expected (Video 3.3).

Step 6. Adjusting the Animation.

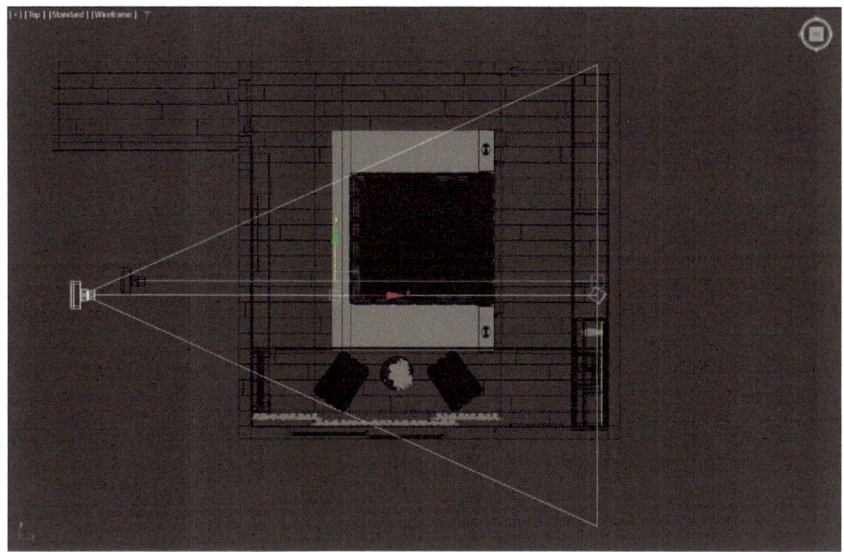

Figure 3.7

New position of Camera 002 at Frame 90 in the Top viewport.

Figure 3.8

Camera002 Viewport at Frame 90.

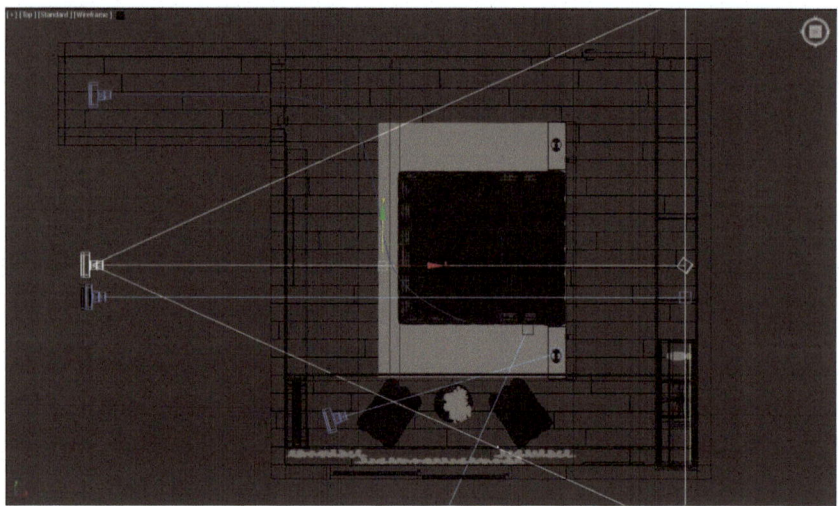

Figure 3.9

Camera002 Viewport at Frame 90.

The camera's movement covers a long distance relative to a 3second animation, which can make the motion appear too fast. To create a more natural pace, you can either extend the timeline or adjust the starting position of the camera. Here's how to finetune the animation:

1. Select both Camera002 and Camera002.Target.
2. Move the Time Slider to Frame 0.
3. Turn on Auto Key to record your adjustments.
4. Move the camera and its target to new starting positions as illustrated in Figures 3.9 and 3.10. This change reduces the distance covered during the animation.
5. Play the animation to verify that the movement now appears smooth and natural.

As mentioned in the previous section, Camera 002 has Camera Clipping enabled. When positioning the camera, ensure it does not cut through any objects in the scene. Pay close attention to the Near clipping plane, and adjust the camera's position so that it stays just before intersecting any objects. If the clipping issue persists, fine-tune the Near value to prevent objects from being visually cut while maintaining a clear and accurate view of the scene.

Figure 3.10

Camera002 Viewport at Frame 90.

3.1.3 Animating the Camera Using the Camera Navigation Controls

To animate the camera, apart from using the Transform Commands like Select & Move or Select & Rotate, you can also utilize the Camera Navigation controls, which provide additional flexibility in setting up camera movement. The choice of control method directly affects the animation style.

Among the Camera Navigation controls, Dolly allows you to move the camera forward or backward. You can dolly the camera, the target, or both, depending on the desired effect – whether pulling the viewer into a scene, creating a zoom-like effect, or adjusting framing without changing perspective. Roll Camera rotates the camera around its viewing axis, often used to create dynamic, unsettling, or stylized shots. Field-of-View (FOV) adjustments change the camera's perspective, widening or narrowing the frame without physically moving the camera, useful for exaggerating depth or focusing attention. Trucking moves the camera laterally while maintaining a consistent distance from the subject, making it ideal for tracking motion. Orbit Camera moves around a focal point, allowing for smooth rotations around an object, often used in product visualizations or architectural walkthroughs.

Each of these movements plays a unique role in guiding the viewer's eye, enhancing storytelling, and setting the emotional tone of an animation.

3.1.3.1 Step-by-Step Example: Animating the Position of the Camera Using Orbit Camera

Step 1. Create a New Camera & Set the Camera Viewport.
1. Create a new camera as seen in Figures 3.11, where the target of the camera is on the coffee table accessories.
2. Switch the viewport to the new camera. Click on the viewport name label, Camera 002, and select Camera 03 from the dropdown menu (Figure 3.12).

Step 2. Animate the Camera.
1. Move the Time Slider at Frame 0.
2. Enable Auto Key.
3. Move the Time Slider at Frame 90.
4. With the Camera 003 viewport active, enable the Orbit Camera command from the Camera Navigation controls (Figure 3.13).
5. Drag the cursor to the right to change the perspective as seen in Figure 3.14.
6. Disable Auto Key.

Step 3. Test the Animation.

Play the animation to ensure that the camera moves as expected.

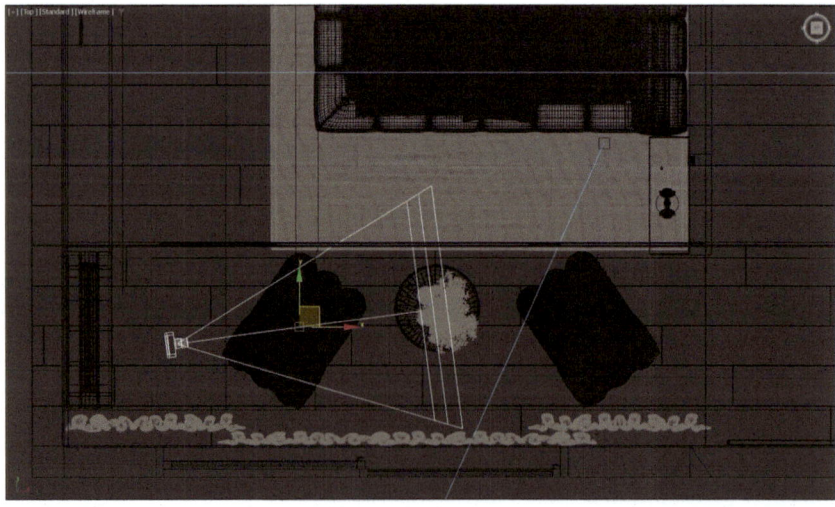

Figure 3.11

New camera placement in the Top viewport.

Camera 003 viewport.

Enabling Orbit Camera.

3.2 Animating the Camera Settings

In this section, the focus shifts to animating the camera settings to create dynamic effects. By adjusting properties such as the focal length, the camera clipping, or the depth of field, it is possible to enhance the storytelling and draw attention to specific elements in the scene. Through three practical examples, this section demonstrates how to animate these settings effectively to bring more depth and creativity to your animations.

Camera03 Viewport at Frame 90.

3.2.1 Step-by-Step Example: Animating the Camera Focal Length

Step 1. Clone the Camera.
1. Select Camera 01.
2. Right-click and choose Clone.
3. In the Clone Options window, select Copy.

Step 2. Switch to the New Camera.
1. In the Camera 003 viewport, click on the name label, Camera 003.
2. From the dropdown menu, select Cameras > Camera 004.

Step 3. Select the Camera and the Target.
1. Press H to open the Select From Scene dialog box.
2. Choose Camera 004 and Camera 004.Target and press OK (Figure 3.15).

Step 4. Clear Existing Keyframes.
Delete all keyframes for Camera 004 from the Timeline to ensure a clean start for the animation.

Step 5. Animate the Camera.
1. Select Camera 004 (not the target).
2. Enable Auto Key.
3. Move the Time Slider to Frame 90.
4. In the Modify Panel:

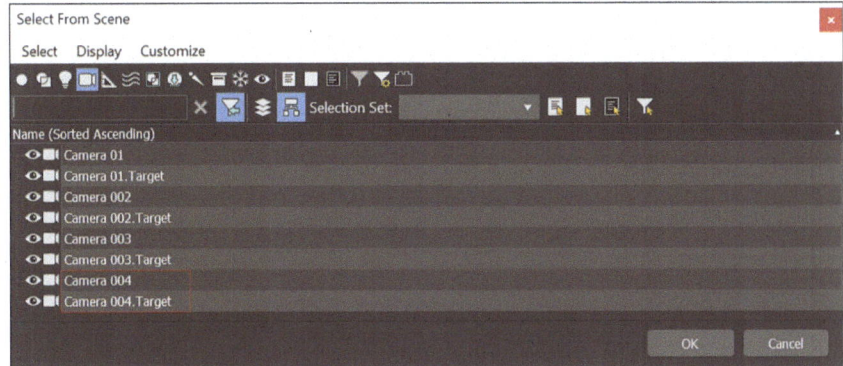

Figure 3.15

Selecting both the camera and the target using the Select From Scene window.

Figure 3.16

Focal length is set to 47 mm at Frame 90.

- If you use Corona, locate the Photographic parameters rollout and set the Focal l. (mm) to 47 (Figure 3.16). A red bracket will appear next to the setting, indicating that it is being animated (Figure 3.17 – left).

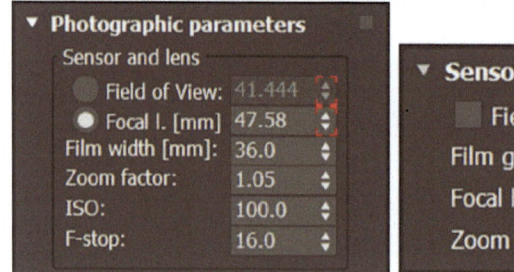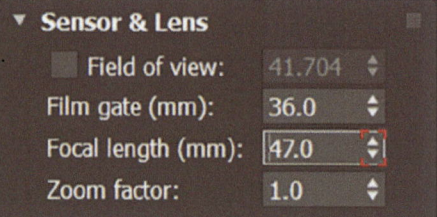

Figure 3.17

The red bracket next to Focal length indicates that the setting is being animated.

- If you use V-Ray, locate the Sensor & Lens rollout and set the Focal length (mm) to 47. A red bracket will appear next to the setting, indicating that it is being animated (Figure 3.17 – right).
5. Turn off Auto Key to stop recording changes.

Step 6. Test the Animation.

Press Play to view the animation (Video 3.4). Observe how the focal length changes over time, creating a zoom-in effect while the camera remains stationary.

3.2.2 Step-by-Step Example: Animating Camera Clipping

Instead of creating a new camera, for this example, you will update the animation of Camera 01.

Step 1. Adjust Existing Keyframes.
1. Select Camera 01.
2. Enable Auto Key.
3. Move the Time Slider to Frame 90.
4. Drag the camera further to the front, as illustrated in Figure 3.18. The Near Clipping Plane intersects the bed. This results in the bed appearing cut at the bottom part in the camera viewport and that part will render black (Figure 3.19).

Step 2. Adjust the Camera Clipping.
1. With the Camera 01 selected, go to the Modify Panel and to
   - the Environment & Clipping rollout, if you use Corona.
   - the Clipping & Environment rollout, if you use V-Ray.
2. Reduce the Near (clipping plane) value to 265 cm or any value necessary so that the Near clipping plane does not intersect the bed (or the armchair) (Figures 3.20 and 3.21).
3. Turn off Auto Key to stop recording changes.

Step 3. Test the Animation.

Press Play to view the animation (Video 3.5).

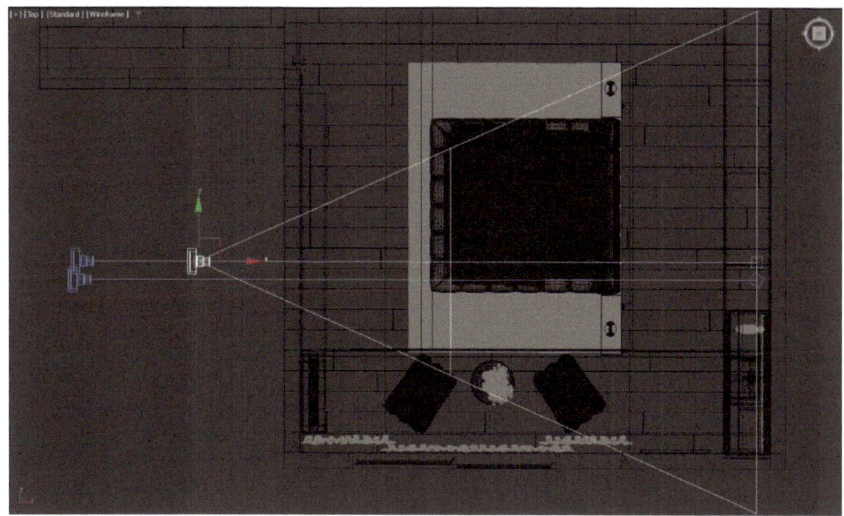

Figure 3.18

Reposition the camera, so that the Near clipping plane intersects the bed.

Figure 3.19

The bed appearing cut in the camera viewport.

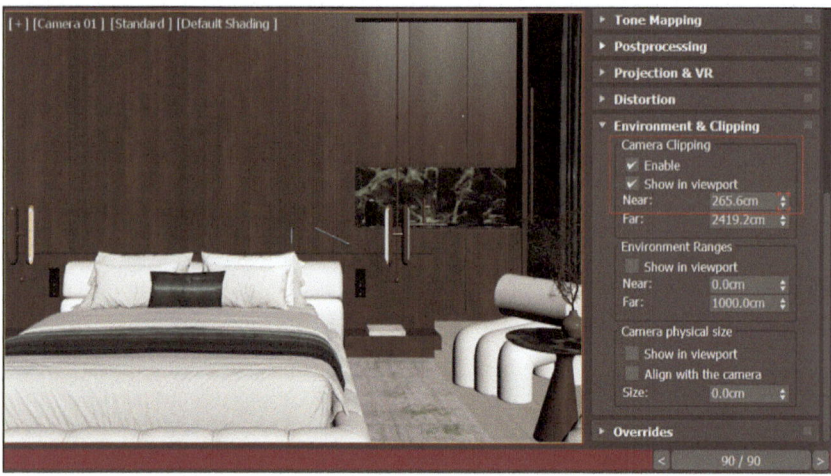

Adjusting the Near value in Corona, so that the bed does not get cut by the clipping planes.

Figure 3.21

Adjusting the Near clipping plane value in V-Ray.

3.2.3 Step-by-Step Example: Animating Depth of Field (DoF)

First, it is important to understand what depth of field (DoF) is. DoF refers to the portion of a scene that appears sharp and in focus. In 3D rendering and animation, DoF simulates how a real-world camera lens works, creating a blurred background or foreground while keeping the subject sharp. This effect enhances realism and directs the viewer's attention to specific elements in the scene.

In the following example, you will animate the DoF effect in the bedroom, gradually shifting the focus from the table accessories to the pendant over the right nightstand.

Unlike the other examples explored so far, understanding the DoF animation requires rendering the animation itself, as it cannot be understood through the preview. The rendering settings will be covered in Chapter 5. For now, the focus will be on preparing the animation, with the rendering process completed in Chapter 5 to view the final result.

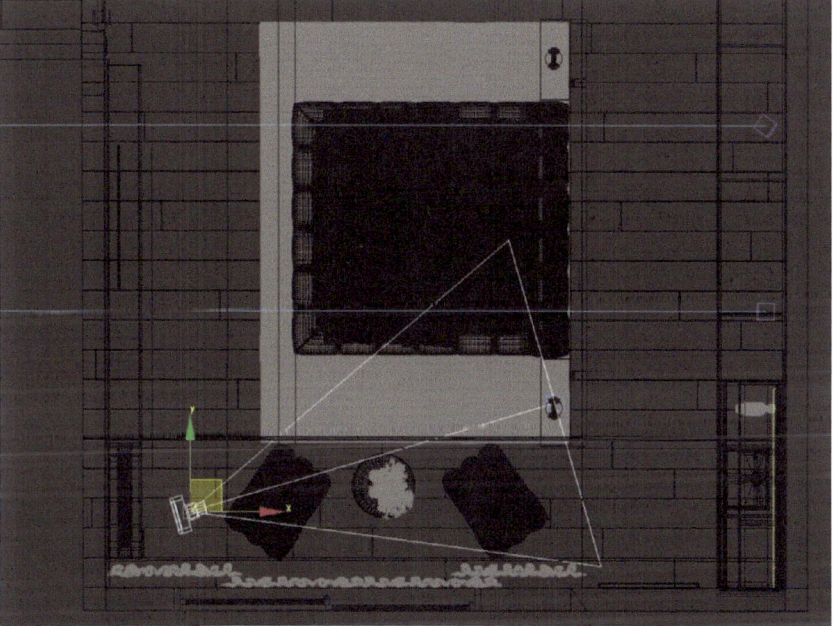

Figure 3.22

Setting a new camera on the floor plan to capture the table accessories and the nightstand pendant.

Step 1. Create a New Camera.
1. Create a new camera.
2. Place it at an angle that captures the table accessories and the night-stand pendant, as illustrated in Figures 3.22 and 3.23.

Step 2. Enable Depth of Field.

Figure 3.23

Camera 005 viewport.

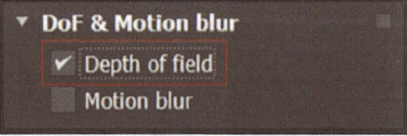

Figure 3.24

Activating Depth of Field in Corona (left) and V-Ray (right).

1. Select the camera.
2. Navigate to the Modify Panel, and locate the DOF & Motion Blur rollout:
   - For Corona users: Check the Enable box under the Depth of Field section (Figure 3.24 – left).
   - For V-Ray users: Check the Depth of field box (Figure 3.24 – right).

Figure 3.25

New camera that captures the table accessories and the nightstand lamp.

Step 3. Do a Test Render.
1. Produce a draft render to understand DoF.
2. Although DoF is enabled the render still appears sharp (Figure 3.25). You need to adjust the F-stop (Corona) or F-Number (V-Ray) values, along with the camera target distance, for the effect to take place.

Step 4. Define the Initial Focus.
1. Set the F-stop/F-Number
   – Adjust the F-stop (Corona) or F-Number (V-Ray) to 2 (Figure 3.26).
   – Lower values (i.e., 2) create a stronger blur effect.
   – Higher values (i.e., 16) produce a subtler blur.
2. Adjust the Focus Distance:
   – For Corona, go to the DOF & Motion Blur rollout. Enable Override focus, and adjust the Value so that the focus plane aligns with the table accessories (Figure 3.27). This way the accessories will be the sharpest element in the render.
   – For V-Ray, go to the Basic & Display rollout. Enable Focus distance, and set the value to position the focus plane on the table accessories (Figure 3.28).
3. Produce a render to check the adjusted DoF (Figure 3.29).

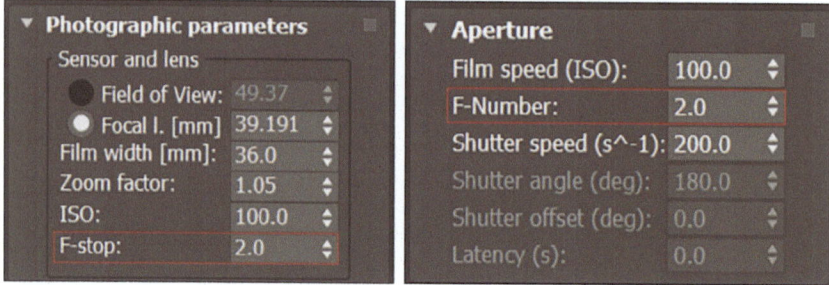

Figure 3.26

Setting the F-stop (left) and F-Number (right) to 2.

Figure 3.27

Enabling Override focus and adjusting the Value in Corona.

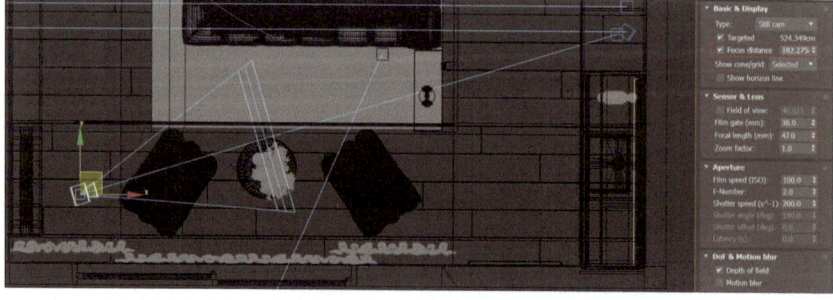

Figure 3.28

Enabling Focus distance and setting the value in V-Ray.

Step 5. Animate the Focus Distance.
1. Select the camera.
2. Move the Time Slider to Frame 0, and enable Auto Key to begin recording changes.

Figure 3.29
Render with F-stop/F-Number set to 2 and the focus on the table accessories.

3. Move the Time Slider to Frame 90, and adjust the Focus Value (Corona) or Focus distance (V-Ray) so that the focus shifts to the nightstand pendant's position (Figures 3.30 and 3.31).
   - A red bracket will appear around the value, indicating that the parameter is being animated.
4. Disable Auto Key to stop recording changes.

Step 6. Check the Depth of Field (DoF).
1. Move the Time Slider to Frame 90.
2. Produce a render to see the adjusted DoF at this frame (Figure 3.32).

Step 7. Play the Animation.
Press Play to preview the animation.
- At the camera viewport, you will notice no difference. As mentioned at the beginning of this exercise, you need to render this animation to understand the gradual change in the DoF (see Chapter 5).
- If you check the preview animation on the Top viewport, you will see how the focus shifts from the table accessories to the nightstand pendant (Video 3.6).

By animating the Depth of Field, the scene gains a cinematic quality, drawing the viewer's attention naturally to key elements like the accessories and the pendant. This technique adds depth and professionalism to your animations.

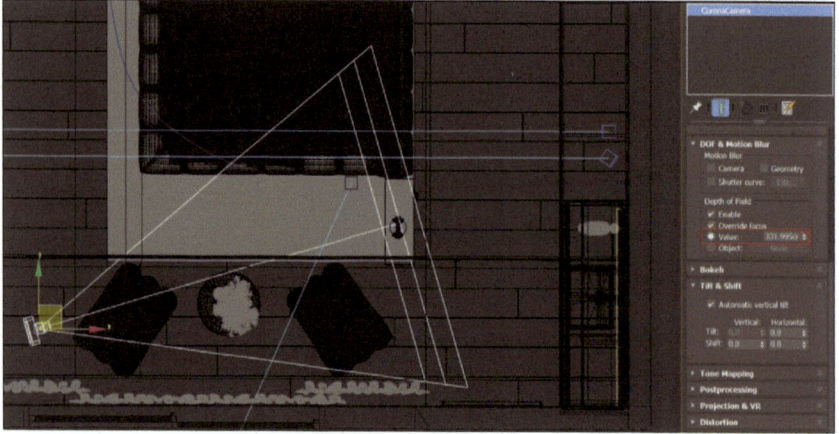

Figure 3.30

Adjusting the focus Value at Frame 90 to align with the nightstand pendant (Corona).

Figure 3.31

Adjusting the Focus distance at Frame 90 to align with the nightstand pendant (V-Ray).

3.3 Walkthrough

In this section, the focus is on creating a walkthrough animation, where the camera moves along a predefined path to simulate walking through a scene. This technique is essential for showcasing architectural designs, interior spaces, or large environments in a dynamic and immersive way. By animating the camera along a path, you can guide the viewer's journey through the scene, highlighting key features and creating a natural flow of movement.

Figure 3.32

Render at Frame 90 showing the adjusted depth of field with the focus on the nightstand pendant.

3.3.1 Step-by-Step Example: Creating a Walkthrough Animation

Step 1. Create a New Camera.

1. Create a new camera and place it at the hallway, as seen in Figure 3.33.
2. In the Viewport display rollout turn off the Targeted option (Figure 3.34). When you want to constraint a camera to follow a path, the target must be disabled.
3. Disable the Depth of Field and the Camera Clipping (Figures 3.35 and 3.36). If you choose to keep the clipping planes enabled, ensure that the camera does not intersect any objects as it moves.

Step 2. Create the Path.

1. Navigate to the Create Panel > Shapes > Splines and select Line (Figure 3.37).
2. Hold the Shift key, and click to define the path for the camera (Figure 3.38). Initially, the path will appear as straight segments.

Step 3. Curve the Path.

1. Select the Line, and go to the Modify Panel.
2. Expand the Line settings under the Modifier List by clicking the arrow, and select Vertex (Figure 3.39).

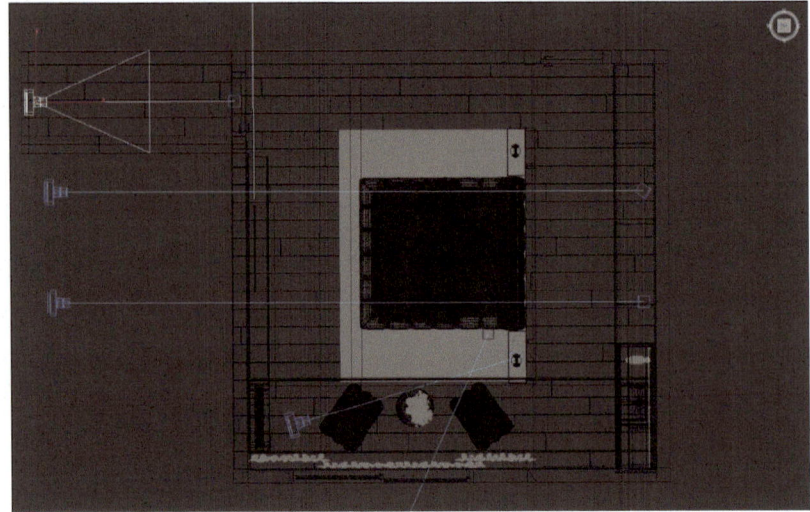

Figure 3.33

Position of the new camera.

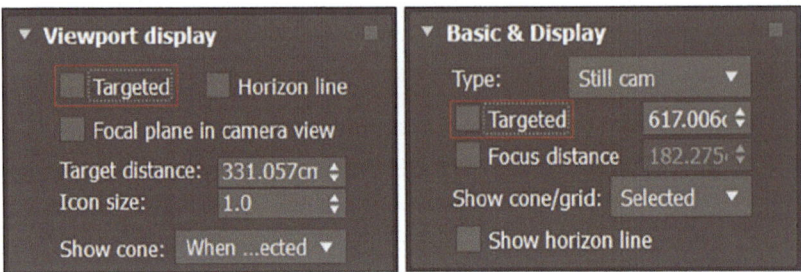

Figure 3.34

Disabling the Targeted option in the new camera settings in Corona (left) and in V-Ray (right).

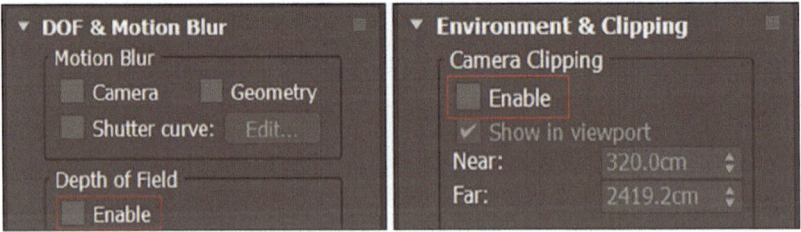

Figure 3.35

Disabling the depth of field and camera clipping in the new Corona camera settings.

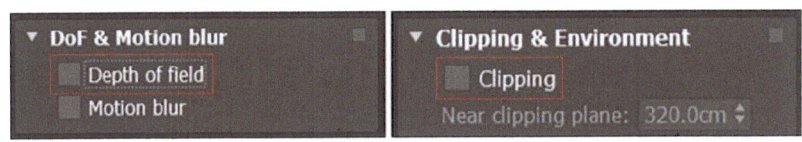

Figure 3.36

Disabling the depth of field and camera clipping in the new V-Ray camera settings.

Splines

▼ **Object Type**

AutoGrid

✔ Start New Shape

Line	Rectangle
Circle	Ellipse
Arc	Donut
NGon	Star
Text	Helix
Egg	Section
Freehand	

Figure 3.37

Enabling the Line command to draw the camera path.

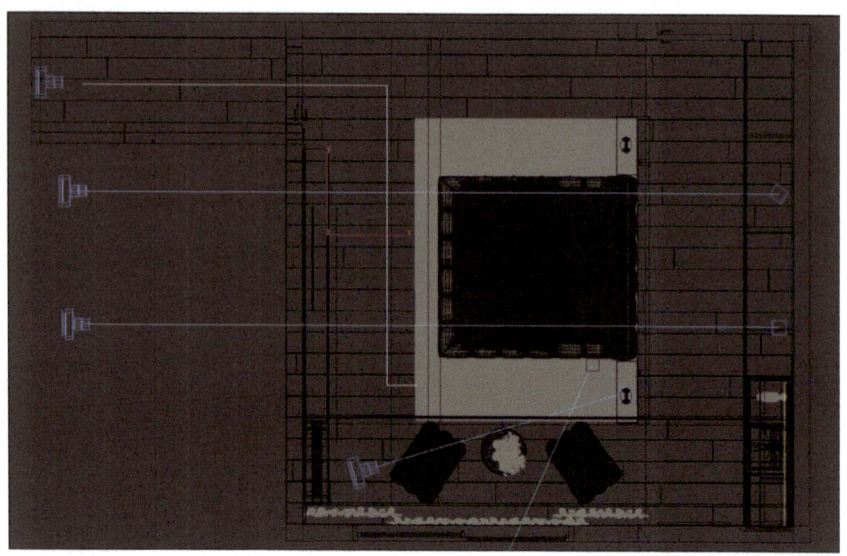

Figure 3.38

The camera path.

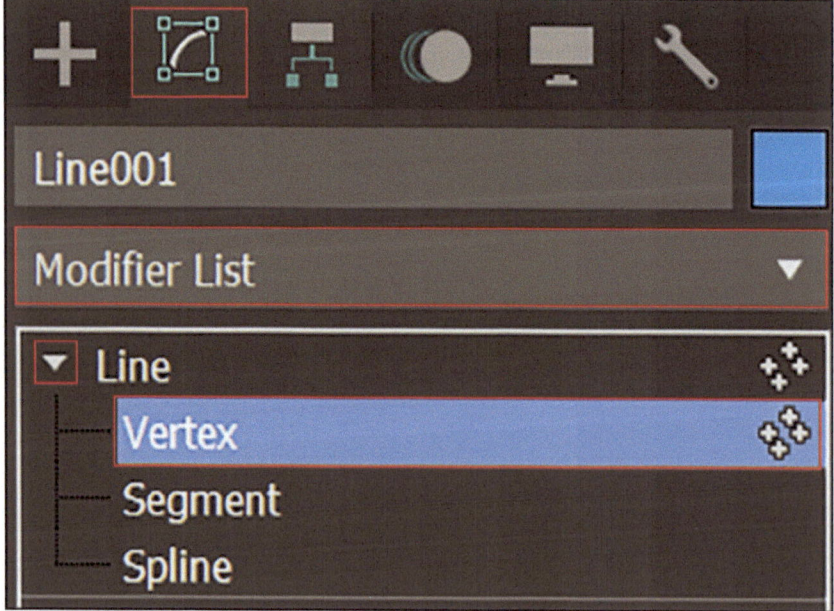

Figure 3.39

Activating Vertex.

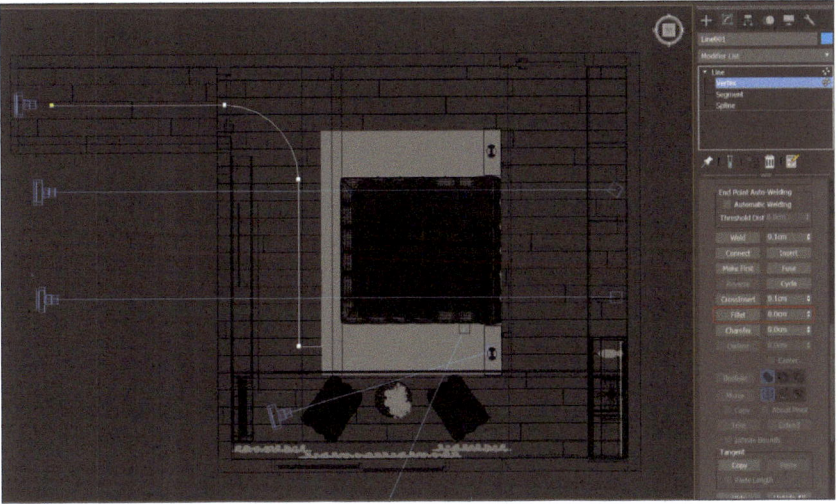

Figure 3.40

Curving the first corner using Fillet.

3. Choose the vertex you want to curve, and use the Fillet setting to curve the corners (Figure 3.40).

4. Repeat for all vertices to create smooth transitions between path segments (Figure 3.41). Then, disable Vertex.

Step 4. Refine the Path.

Under the Line's parameters, set the Interpolation value to 100 to ensure that the curved sections of the path are smooth (Figures 3.42 and 3.43).

Step 5. Adjust the Animation Duration.

1. Since the path is quite long, increase the animation duration, so that the camera will not move too fast. Open the Time Configuration window.

2. Set the Length to 180 frames for a total duration of 6 seconds (at 30 fps) (Figure 3.44).

Step 6. Align the Path.

Select the path, and move it upward so that it aligns with the height of the camera in the scene (Figure 3.45).

Step 7. Assign the Path to the Camera.

1. Select the camera and go to the Motion Tab.

2. Under Parameters, select Position (Figure 3.46).

3. Click on the Assign Controller button, <Icon 3.1 here>, and from the pop-up list, choose Path Constraint. Click OK (Figure 3.47).

4. In the Path Parameters, click the Add Path button (Figure 3.48) and select the line you created.

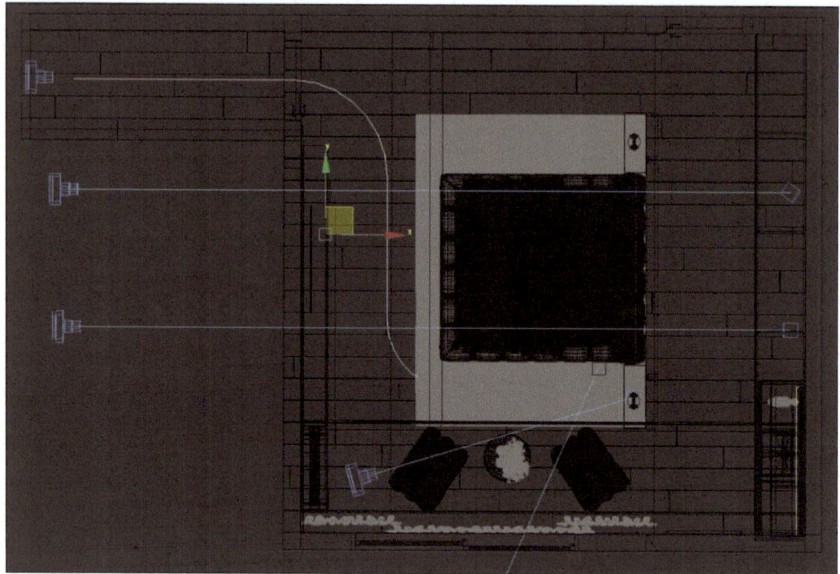

Figure 3.41

Curving all corners for a smooth path.

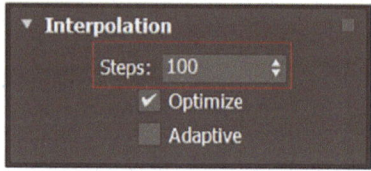

Figure 3.42

Set the Interpolation to 100 to ensure smoothness on the curved sections.

Step 8. Preview the Animation.
1. Play the animation to preview the camera's movement (Video 3.7).
2. If the camera is not facing the path's direction, enable the Follow option in the Path Constraint Parameters (Figure 3.49).

Step 9. Animate the Door to Open.
1. Now the camera passes through the closed door. To open the door, select it and drag the Time Slider to Frame 0. Activate Set Key, and click on Set Keys to set the first keyframe of the door at the closed position.
2. Drag the time slider to Frame 30. At this frame, the camera has approached the door.

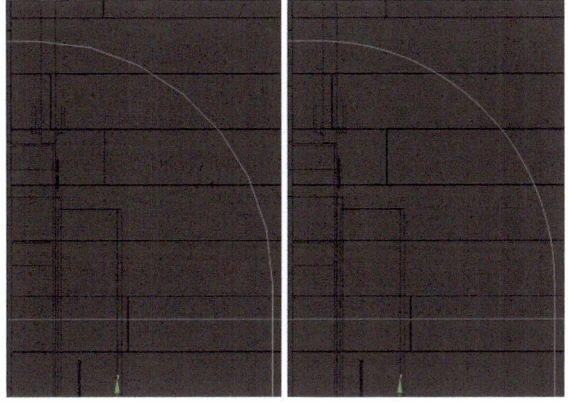

Figure 3.43

Interpolation Steps: 6 (left) and Interpolation Steps: 100 (right).

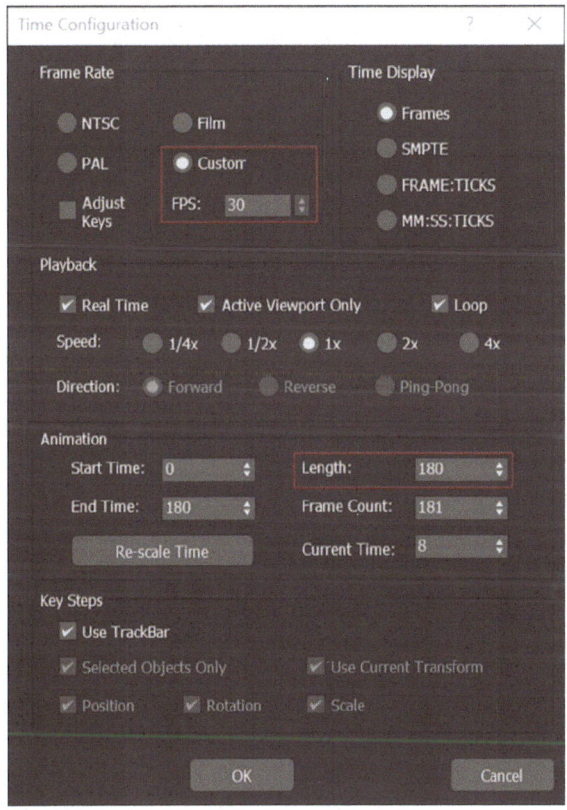

Figure 3.44

The Length of the animation set to 180 frames.

Figure 3.45

Aligning the path to the camera's height.

Figure 3.46

Selecting Position under Parameters.

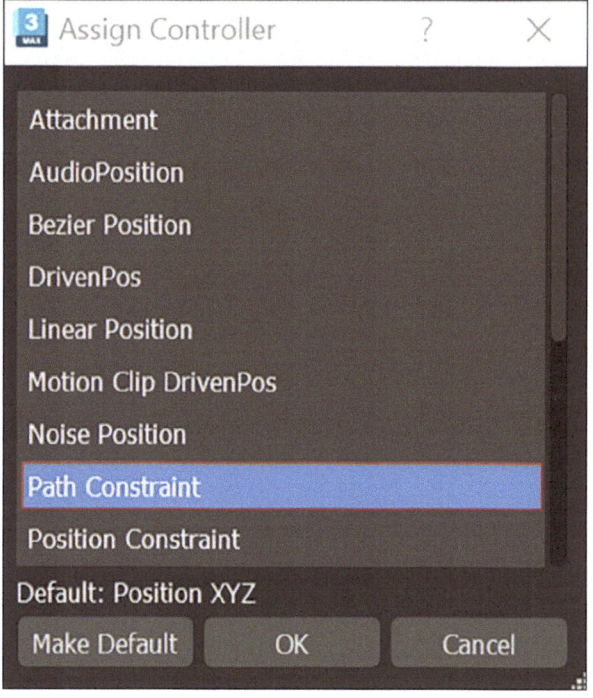

Figure 3.47

Selecting Path Constraint.

3. Enable the Select & Rotate tool, and rotate the door 90° to open (Figure 3.50).
4. Click on the Set Keys button to keyframe the change.
5. Disable Set Keys.

Step 10. Preview the Animation.

Play the animation to preview the camera's movement in combination with the door opening (Video 3.8).

Step 11. Final Adjustments.

1. Refine the path or camera settings as needed to achieve the desired result (Figure 3.51).
2. Test the animation to ensure smooth camera movement and realistic walkthrough result (Video 3.9).

By following these steps, the camera will smoothly move along the path, creating an immersive walkthrough animation. This technique is particularly useful for architectural visualizations, allowing viewers to explore spaces dynamically.

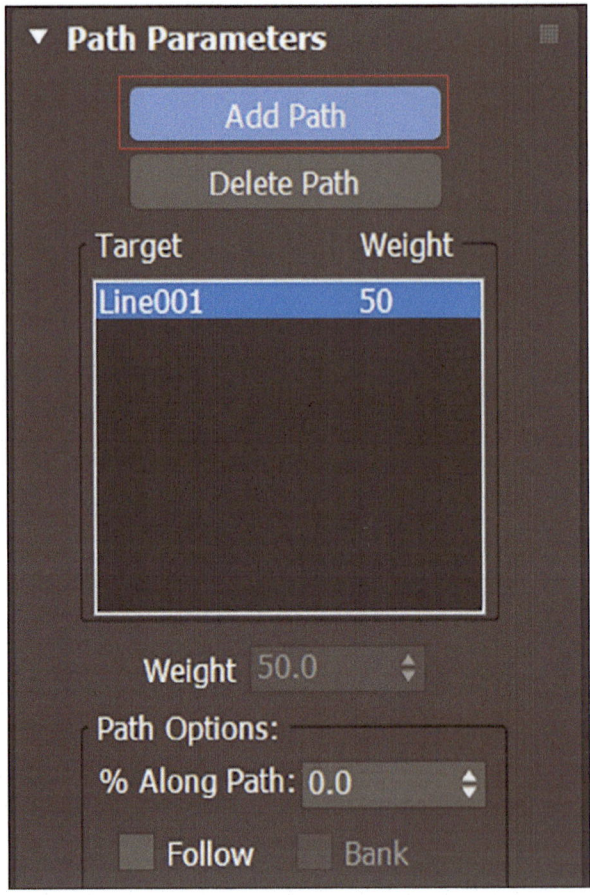

Figure 3.48

Clicking the Add Path button and selecting the line.

Figure 3.49

Enabling the Follow checkbox.

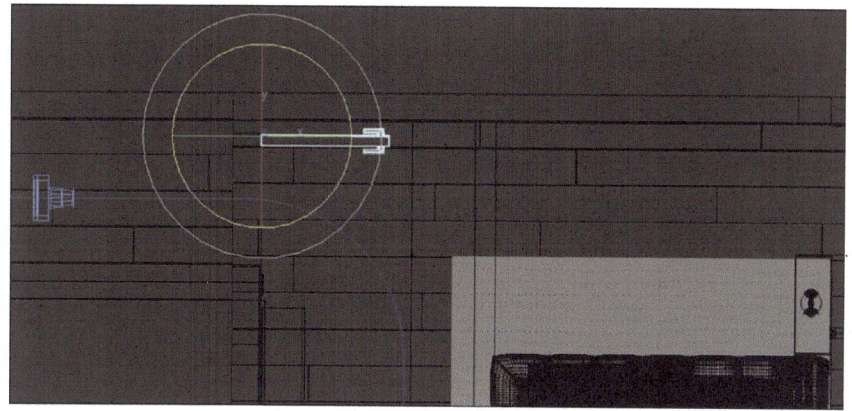

Figure 3.50

Rotating the door by 90° at Frame 30.

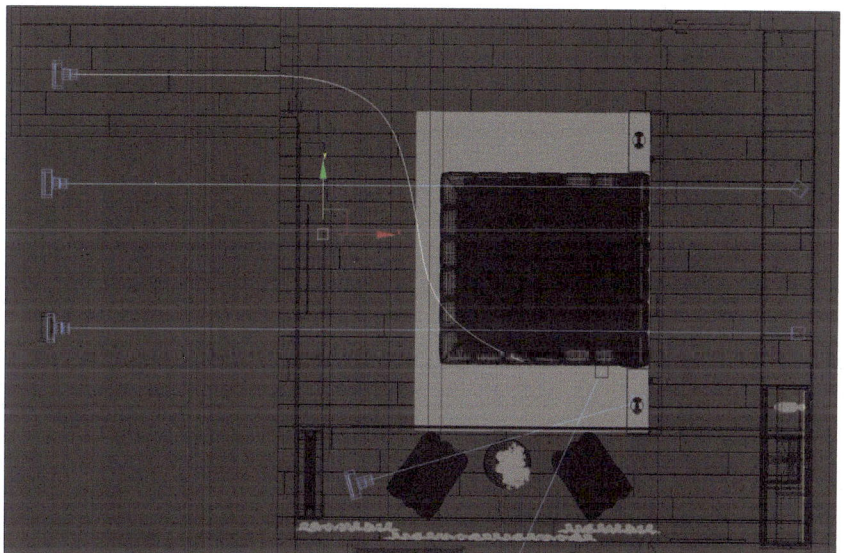

Figure 3.51

Refined path.

4

Lighting Animation

4.1 Light Intensity Animation

Animating light intensity can simulate real-world effects like lights turning on gradually or varying brightness throughout a sequence, crucial for storytelling and atmosphere. This section explores how to modify and animate light intensity step by step.

To begin, open the file Chapter 4, which contains the bedroom interior scene used for this exercise. Rendering the scene in its current state produces an image like the one shown in Figure 4.1.

The first light to animate is the LED light at the bar area. The goal is to create an animation where the light transitions from being turned off to being fully illuminated. The animation is set to a total length of 120 frames with a frame rate of 30 fps, resulting in a 4-second animation (Figure 4.2).

4.1.1 Step-by-Step Example: Animating the Intensity of the Pendant

Step 1. Select the Light.

    1. Click on the Selection Filter dropdown, and choose Lights (Figure 4.3 – left). This restriction allows you to select only lights from the scene.

DOI: 10.1201/9781003651222-4

Render of the bedroom interior scene used as an example in this chapter.

2. Click on the light.
3. Alternatively, press the H key on your keyboard to open the Select From Scene dialog box. From the list, select the bar light and click OK (Figure 4.3 – right).

Step 2. Animate the Intensity of the Light.

1. In the Modify Panel, in the Corona Light rollout, set the Intensity to 0 (Figure 4.4).
2. Drag the Time Slider to Frame 0 on the Timeline.
3. Activate Auto Key to start recording the changes.
4. Drag the Time Slider to Frame 120.
5. In the Corona Light rollout, set the Intensity to 15. A red bracket appears at the Intensity value indicating that this parameter is being animated (Figure 4.5).
6. Disable Auto Key to complete the animation.

Step 3. Preview the Animation.

Light animations cannot be previewed directly in the viewport. To see the results, the animation needs to be rendered, a process that will be explored in Chapter 5. However, by clicking the Play button on the Timeline, it is possible to observe how the Intensity value transitions smoothly from Frame 0 to Frame 120 (Video 4.1).

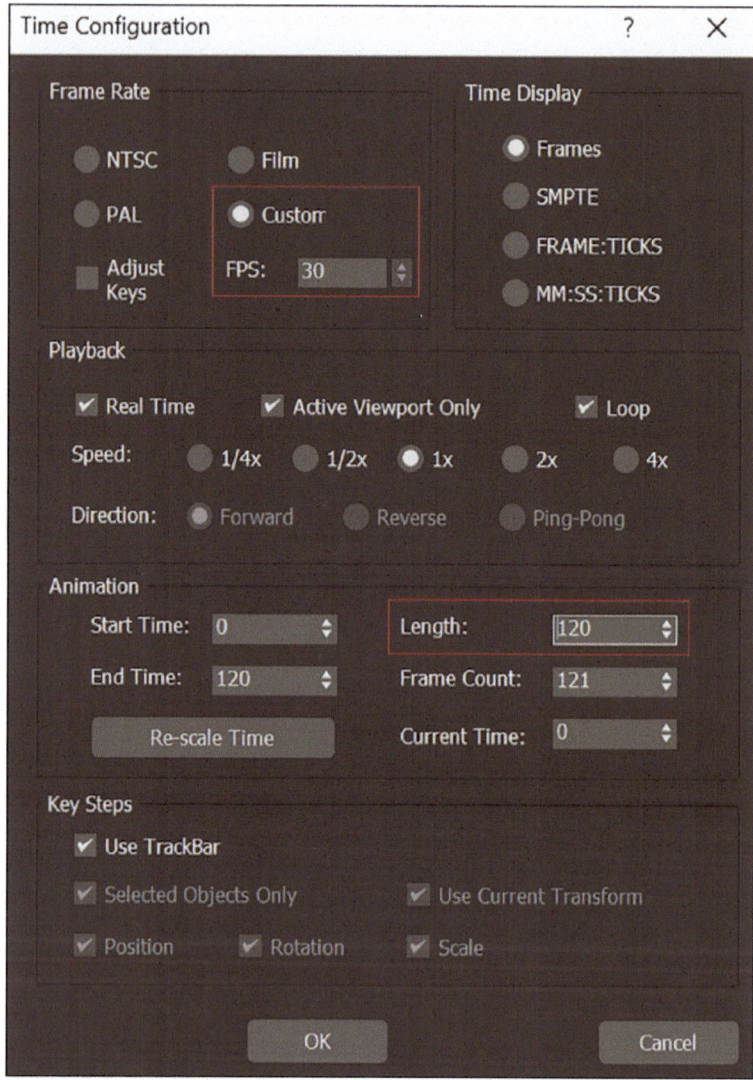

Figure 4.2

The Time Configuration with 30fps and 120 frames Length.

In cases where the animation cannot be previewed, but rendering is required, it is recommended to perform at least two test renders. Render one at Frame 0, where the Intensity is set to 0 (Figure 4.6), and the other at Frame 120 (Figure 4.7), where the Intensity is set to 15. This approach helps to ensure that the desired lighting effect is achieved before rendering the entire animation.

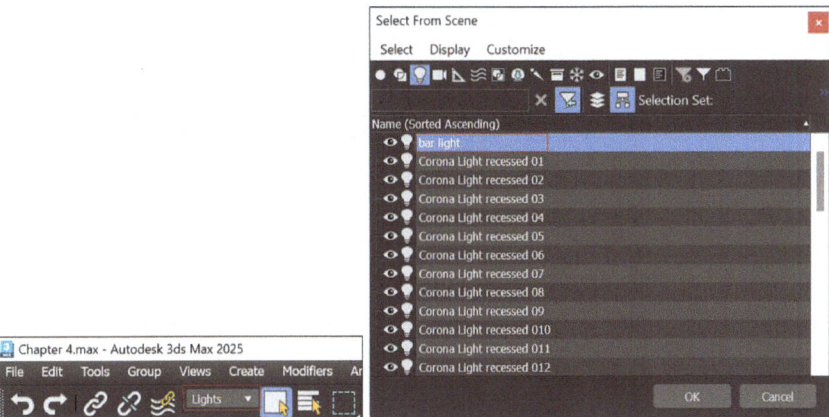

The Selection Filter set to Lights (left) and the Select From Scene dialog box (right).

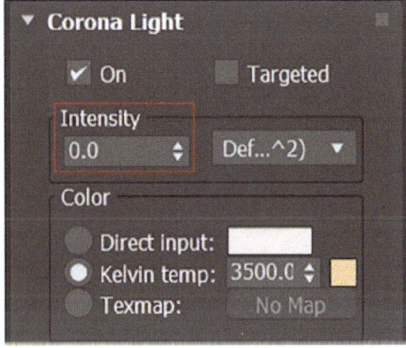

Figure 4.4

Setting the Intensity to 0 for Frame 0.

If you used the Selection Filter to select the light, remember to change it back to All after completing this example to ensure that you can select other objects in the scene.

4.1.2 Step-by-Step Example: Animating the Intensity of the Pendant Lights

Each pendant has two light sources, so there are four lights in total. Since these lights are instances, animating one light will automatically animate all four.

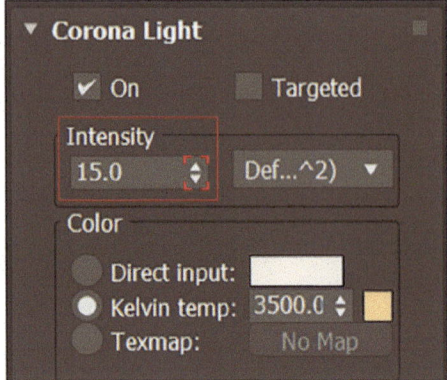

Figure 4.5

The red bracket indicating that the Intensity is being animated.

Figure 4.6

Render at Frame 0 with the bar light Intensity set to 0.

Step 1. Access the Pendant's Lights.
1. Open the group containing the pendant's lights:
   – Select the right pendant.
   – Go to the menu Group, and select Open (Figure 4.8).
2. Click the Selection Filter dropdown, and choose Lights.
3. Click on the right part of the pendant to select its light (Figure 4.9).

Figure 4.7

Render at Frame 120 with the bar light Intensity set to 15.

Figure 4.8

Going to the Group menu to Open the pendant.

Figure 4.9

Selecting the light in the right pendant.

Step 2. Animate the Intensity of the Right Light of the Right Pendant.
1. In the Modify Panel, in the Corona Light rollout, set the Intensity to 0.
2. Drag the Time Slider to Frame 0 on the Timeline.
3. Activate Auto Key.
4. Drag the Time Slider to Frame 120.
5. In the Corona Light rollout, set the Intensity to 100.
6. Disable Auto Key to complete the animation of the selected light.

Step 3. Verify the Other Lights.
1. Select each of the other three lights.
2. In the Modify Panel, confirm that the Intensity value has a red bracket. This indicates that the animation is applied to all instance lights.

Step 4. Preview the Animation.

As mentioned earlier in this chapter, light animations cannot be previewed directly in the viewport. To see the results, the animation needs to be rendered, a process that will be explored in Chapter 5. However, by clicking the Play button on the Timeline, it is possible to observe how the Intensity value of the selected light transitions smoothly from Frame 0 to Frame 120.

It is recommended to perform at least two test renders. Render one at Frame 0, where the Intensity is set to 0 (Figure 4.10), and the other one at Frame 120 (Figure 4.11), where the Intensity is set to 100. This approach

Figure 4.10

Render at Frame 0 with the pendant lights Intensity set to 0.

Figure 4.11

Render at Frame 120 with the pendant lights Intensity set to 50.

helps to ensure that the desired lighting effect is achieved before rendering the entire animation.

By animating the intensity of the lights, the pendant lights achieve a dynamic and realistic lighting effect.

4.2 Color Temperature and Light's Color Animation

Animating color temperature is an effective technique for simulating transitions between different times of day, such as moving from a warm, evening glow to a cool, daylight tone. On the other hand, animating the color of a light is commonly used in decorative lighting, concerts, or artistic visualizations to produce dynamic and visually striking effects. Both techniques offer creative opportunities to enhance the mood and storytelling of a scene.

4.2.1 Step-by-Step Example: Animating the Color Temperature of the Pendants

This example demonstrates how to animate the color temperature of a light, transitioning from a warm glow to a cool white tone.

Step 1. Select the Pendant Lamp Light.
1. Click on the Selection Filter dropdown, and choose Lights.
2. Click on the pendant to select its light.

Step 2. Adjust the Timeline for the Animation.
Since the light already has keyframes, either delete them or extend the Timeline to accommodate the new animation beyond Frame 120.
1. Click the Time Configuration button.
2. Set the Length to 180.

Step 3. Animate the Color Temperature.
1. With the light selected, go to the Modify Panel and locate the Corona Light rollout.
2. Set the Color Temperature to 2,700 K to simulate a warm glow.
3. Drag the Time Slider to Frame 120.
4. Activate Auto Key.
5. Drag the Time Slider to Frame 180.
6. Change the Color Temperature to 6,500 K to simulate a daylight tone.
7. Disable Auto Key to finalize the animation.

Step 4. Preview the Animation.
As with intensity animations, changes in color temperature cannot be previewed directly in the viewport. However, clicking the Play button will display how the Color Temperature value changes over time in the Timeline (Video 4.2).

Produce two draft renders, one at Frame 120 and the other at Frame 180, to confirm the light's color temperature before rendering the full animation (Figures 4.12 and 4.13).

Figure 4.12

Render at Frame 120 with the pendants' light temperature set to 2,700 K.

Figure 4.13

Render at Frame 180 with the pendants' light temperature set to 6,500 K.

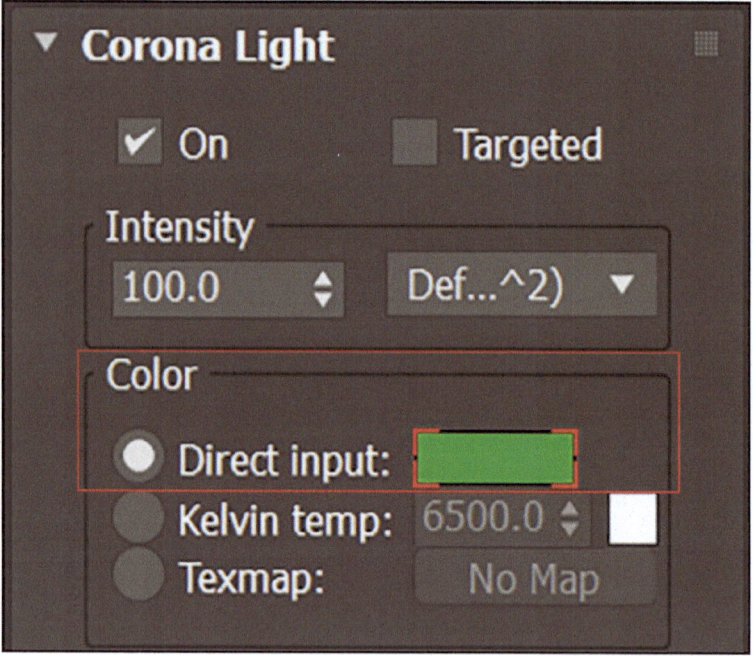

Figure 4.14

Changing the pendant light color to green.

4.2.2 Step-by-Step Example: Animating a Light's Color Change

This example demonstrates a light transitioning through various colors, useful for decorative or artistic lighting setups.

Step 1. Select the Pendant Light.
1. Use the Selection Filter to choose Lights.
2. Select any of the four lights of the pendant since they are instances.

Step 2. Animate the Light's Color.
1. In the Corona Light rollout, set the initial Light Color to green with an RGB value of 0/142/0 (Figure 4.14).
2. Drag the Time Slider to Frame 120, and activate Auto Key.
3. Drag the Time Slider to Frame 150, and change the Light Color to red with an RGB value of 255/0/0 (Figure 4.15 – left).
4. Drag the Time Slider to Frame 180, and change the Light Color to blue with an RGB value of 0/0/255 (Figure 4.15 – right).
5. Disable Auto Key.

Step 3. Preview the Animation.

As with color temperature animations, changes in color cannot be previewed directly in the viewport. However, clicking the Play

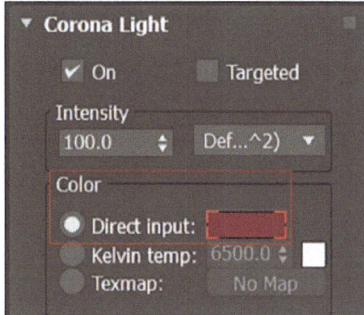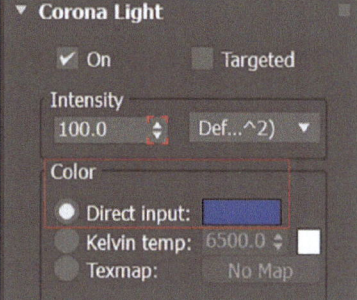

Figure 4.15

Changing the nightstand light color to red (left) and blue (right).

Figure 4.16

Render at Frame 120 with the light color set to green.

button will display how the Color changes over time in the Timeline (Video 4.3).

Produce three draft renders at Frames 120, 150, and 180 to confirm the light's colors: green, red, and blue, respectively, before rendering the full animation (Figures 4.16–4.18).

Figure 4.17

Render at Frame 150 with the light color set to red.

Figure 4.18

Render at Frame 180 with the light color set to blue.

4.3 Sunlight Animation

Animating sunlight in your 3D scenes is an impactful way to bring a design to life. Whether you want to demonstrate how shadows shift across a room or capture the golden glow of a sunset, mastering sunlight animation will elevate your visual storytelling and add realism to your projects.

4.3.1 Step-by-Step Example: Animating the Position of the Sun

Open the file Chapter 6_Sunlight. Inside, you will find Camera 01, positioned near the bed and facing the wardrobe. Rendering the scene will produce an image similar to Figure 4.19, where sunlight gently illuminates the wardrobe. You'll also notice the soft shadows cast by the sheer curtain and the tree outside the bedroom window.

Step 1. Select the Sun.
- Click directly on the sun in the viewport.
- Alternatively, use the Select From Scene dialog box to locate and select it (Figure 4.20).

Figure 4.19

Render of Camera 01.

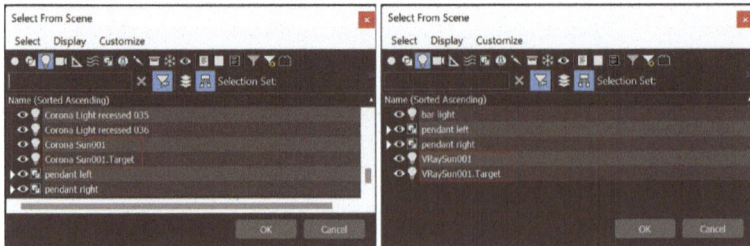

Figure 4.20

Selecting the Corona Sun (left) and the V-RaySun (right) using the Select From Scene dialog box.

Step 2. Animate the Position of the Sun.
1. Enable the Select & Move command.
2. Set the initial keyframe.
    - Move the Time Slider to Frame 0.
    - Enable Auto Key.
3. Move the sun position.
    - Move the Time Slider to Frame 90.
    - With the Camera 01 Viewport active, navigate to the Z field in the Coordinates Display and type −200 (Figure 4.21).
    - Disable Auto Key.

Step 3. Preview the Animation.

As with other lighting animations, changes in the position of the sun cannot be previewed directly in the viewport. However, clicking the Play button will display how the position of the sun lowers over time in the Timeline (Video 4.4).

Produce two draft renders at Frames 0, and 90 to check how the sun casts shadows, before rendering the full animation (Figures 4.22 and 4.23).

This chapter demonstrated various techniques to animate lights from adjusting intensity and color temperature to creating dynamic color transitions. By mastering these methods, you can enhance the realism and visual storytelling of your scenes, bringing a new level of engagement to your projects.

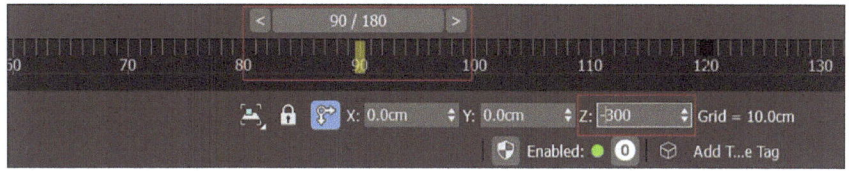

Figure 4.21

Moving the sun position using the Coordinates Display.

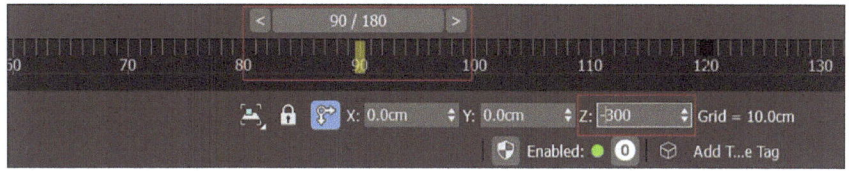

Figure 4.22

Render at Frame 0 with the original position of the sun.

Figure 4.23

Render at Frame 90 with the sun position moved.

5

Rendering Settings for Animation

5.1 Understanding the Rendering Workflow

Before diving into the settings, it is essential to understand the rendering workflow for animations. Rendering an animation means producing multiple frames, each of which is a still image. The settings you choose will affect how these frames are calculated and the time it takes to render them.

5.1.1 Step-by-Step Rendering Workflow

Step 1. Set the Frame Rate.
1. Open the Time Configuration dialog.
2. Set the desired Frame Rate. In the examples explored in the previous chapters, 30 fps was used for smoother motion (Figure 5.1).
3. Click OK to save your settings.

Step 2. Select Active Time Segment for Rendering.
1. Go to the Render Setup dialog (F10).
2. Set the Time Output to Active Time Segment to render the entire Timeline (Figure 5.2), or choose Range to render a specific sequence of frames.

DOI: 10.1201/9781003651222-5

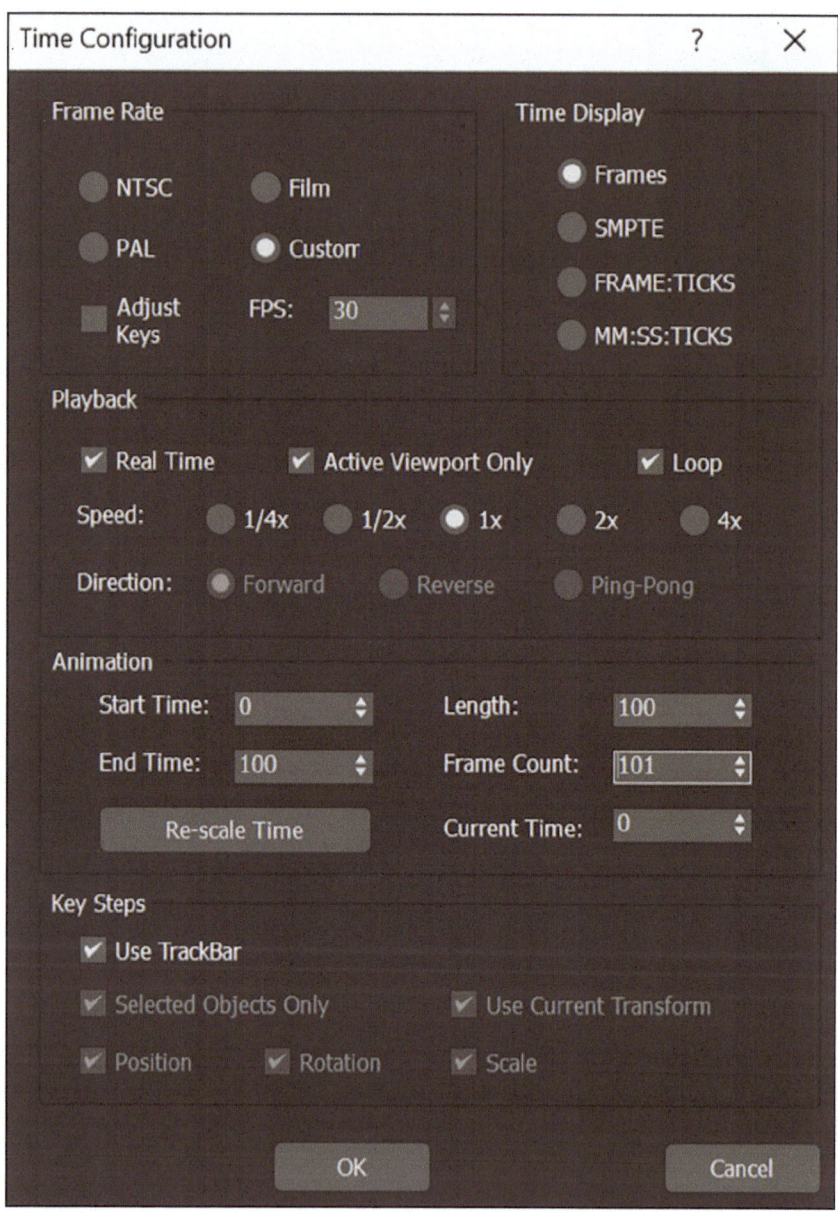

Figure 5.1

Setting the FPS.

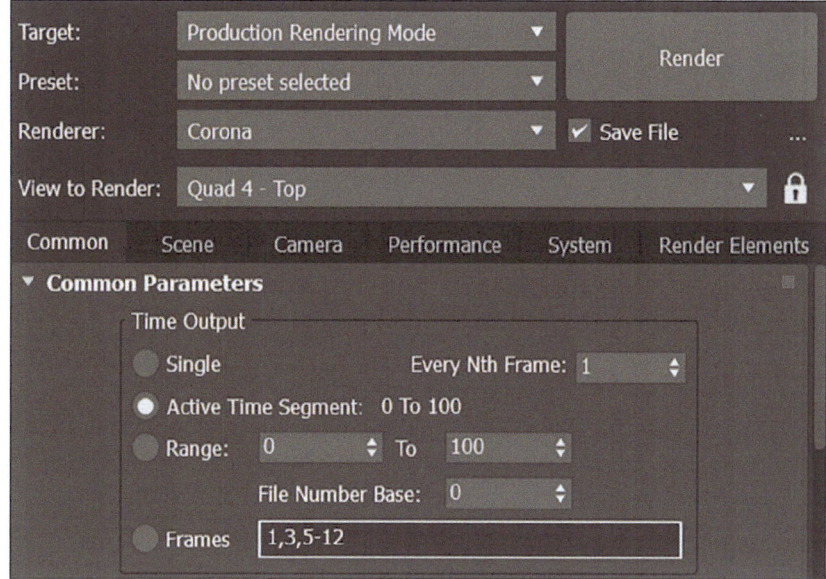

Figure 5.2

Choosing Active Time Segment.

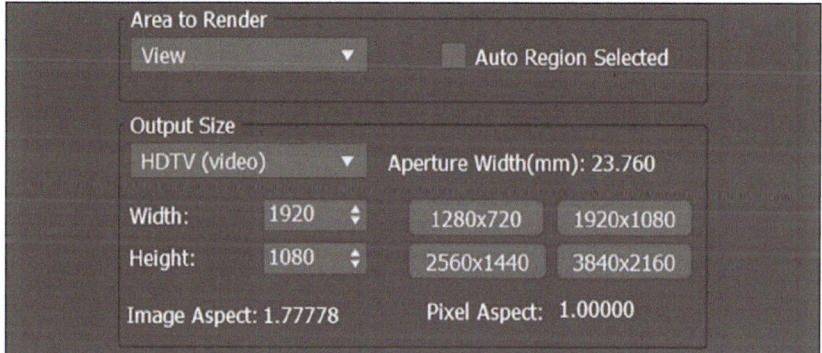

Figure 5.3

Choosing the Output Size.

Step 3. Choose the Resolution.

1. In the Render Setup dialog, under the Common tab, locate the Output Size section.
2. Select a preset resolution (i.e., HD 1920×1080) or manually input custom dimensions (Figure 5.3). Resolution Guidelines:
   - For general presentations and online sharing, use 1,920×1,080.
   - For large screen displays, consider 4K resolution (3,840×2,160).

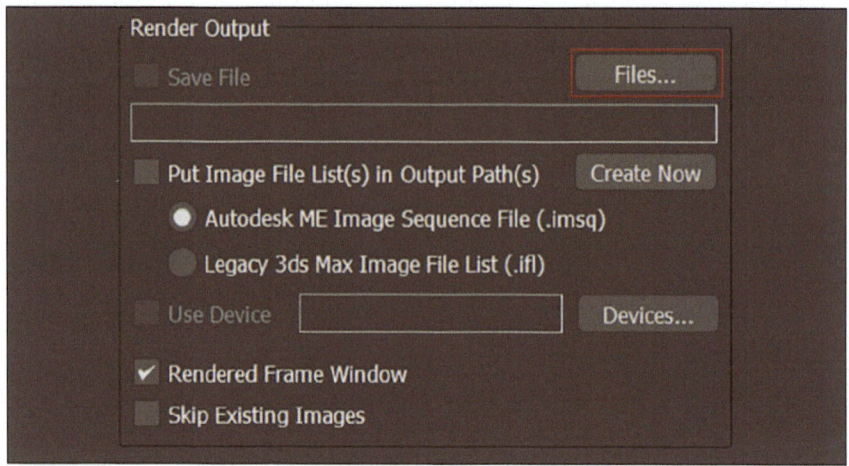

Figure 5.4

Clicking Files... to choose the save location and format.

- For social media posts, adjust the aspect ratio according to the platform requirements. Example: For an Instagram post animation, use a square resolution (i.e., 1,080×1,080).

Step 4. Define the Output Format.

1. In the Common tab navigate to the Render Output section. Click Files... to choose the save location and format (i.e., PNG or EXR) (Figure 5.4).
2. Enter the desired file name, adding an underscore (_) at the end. 3ds Max will automatically number each frame in the sequence.

Consider disabling displacement, if render times are high.

5.2 Rendering Settings in Corona

Step 1. Configure Progressive Rendering.

1. Open the Render Setup dialog, and switch to the Scene tab.
2. Set a pass limit or a noise level limit to control frame quality.
   - A noise level of 4%–5% is acceptable for animations and helps reduce render times (Figure 5.5).

Step 2. Enable Denoising.

1. Go to the Denoising section in the Corona tab.
2. Choose High Quality for the best results in animations.
3. Increase the denoising Amount, if the noise level is higher, i.e., 0.75–0.85 (Figure 5.6).

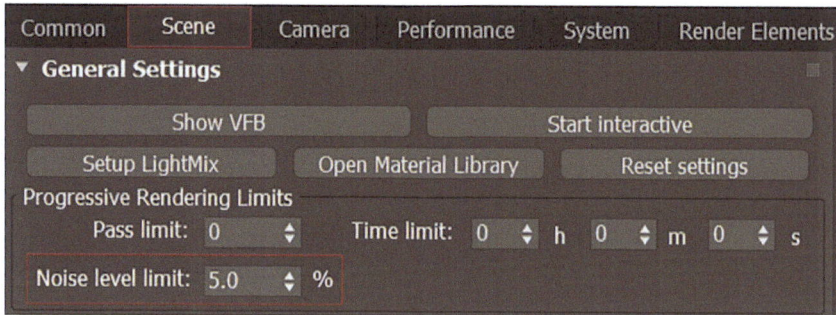

Figure 5.5

Setting the Noise level limit to 5%.

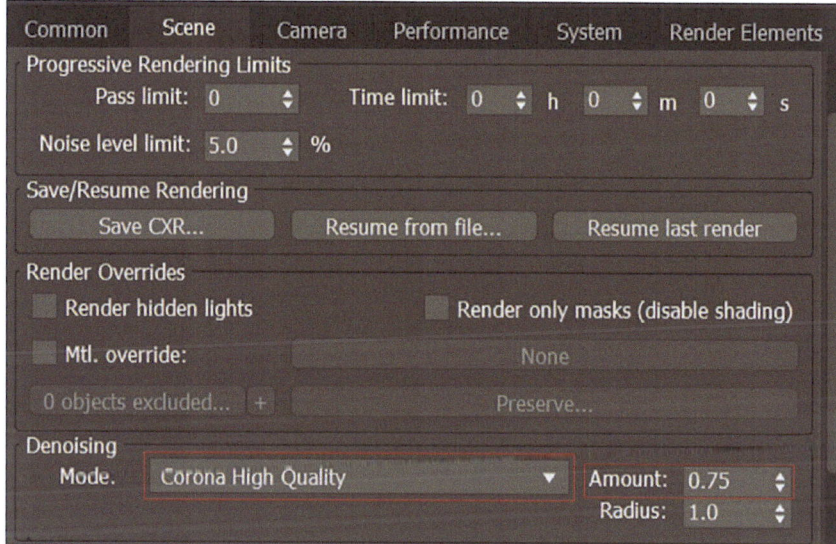

Figure 5.6

Setting the Denoising Mode to Corona High Quality and adjusting the Amount.

Step 3. Set the UHD Cache Mode.
1. Go to the Performance tab and to the UHD Cache rollout.
2. Set the UHD Cache mode to Animation for flicker-free results (Figure 5.7).

5.3 Rendering Settings in V-Ray

Step 1. Setting Up the Render Output.
In Section 5.1, you learned how to save the rendered output. When using V-Ray, you have two options:

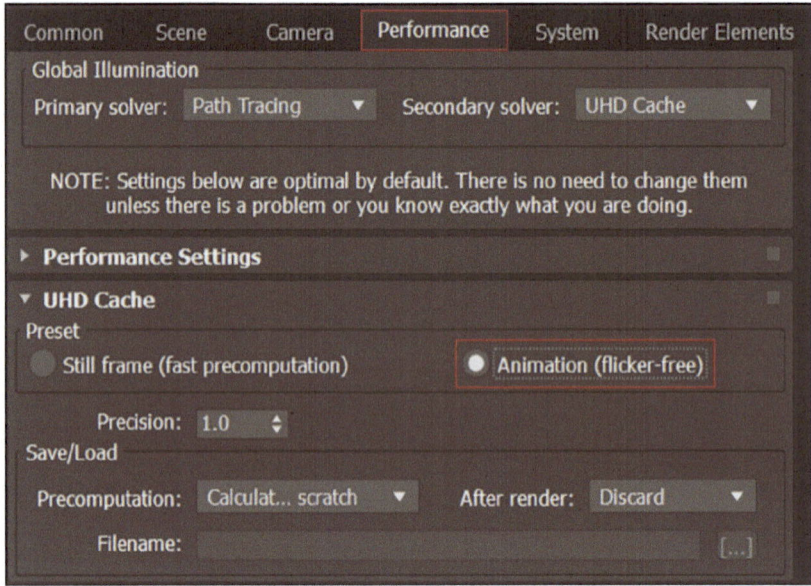

Figure 5.7

Setting the UHD Cache mode to Animation.

– Use the Render Output section in the Common tab. Choose PNG as the file format for optimal quality.
– Navigate to the V-Ray tab and to the Frame Buffer rollout. Enable V-Ray raw image file output, and set the format to EXR for flexibility in post-production (Figures 5.8 and 5.9).

Step 2. Configure the Rendering Settings.
1. Configure the Image Sampler (Antialiasing):
   – When using the Progressive method, it is not recommended to set a maximum render time for animations, as it can cause flickering due to inconsistent noise levels.
   – To prevent this, switch to Bucket Mode for more control.
     o Set Min Subdivs to 1 and Max Subdivs to 24 as a starting point.
     o Set the Noise Threshold to 0.015 to balance quality and render time (Figure 5.10).
2. Adjust the Global Illumination (GI) Settings:
   – Set Light Cache to Animation mode to prevent flickering and light leaks (Figure 5.11).

Step 3. Add Render Elements.
1. Navigate to the Render Elements tab.
2. Add the Denoiser Element. Go to the Advanced Denoiser Parameters rollout, and set it to Generate Elements Only to avoid per-frame

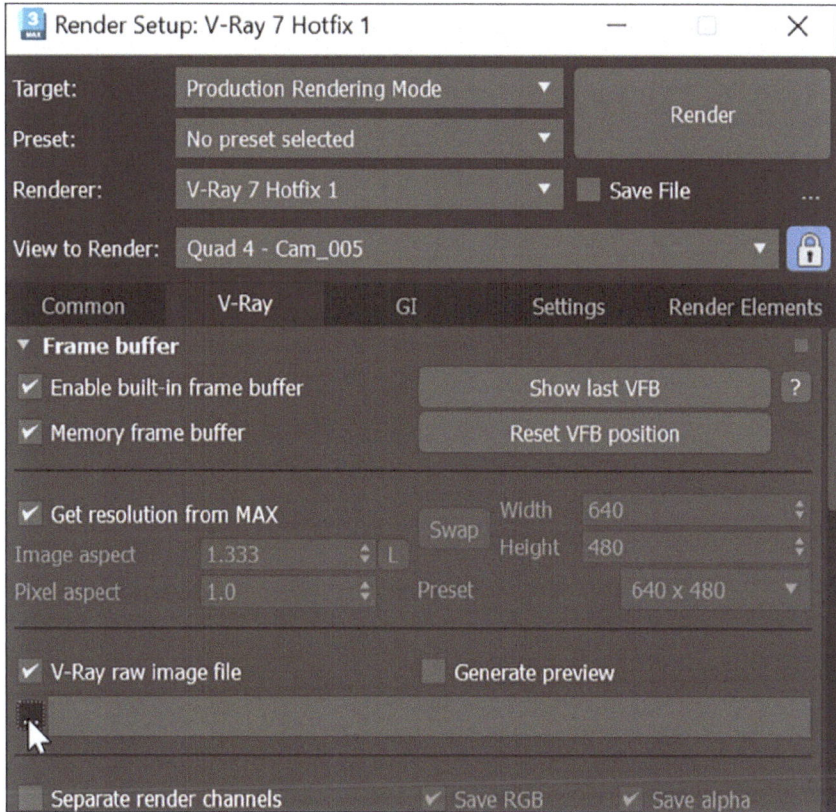

Figure 5.8

Enabling V-Ray raw image file.

inconsistencies (Figure 5.12). This way it does not denoise immediately and you need to use the Denoiser Standalone to compose them.
 – Otherwise, keep the default option, and it will automatically denoise the images.
3. Another Element you could add is BackToBeauty, to get all the passes you need for compositing. It is essential to only add elements that will be used in compositing to avoid large file sizes and increased render times.

Step 4. Denoising the Rendered EXR Sequence.
1. Open the Standalone Denoiser Tool:
 – Type vdenoise in the computer's search bar.
 – Or navigate to the default installation path: C:\Program Files\ Chaos Group\V-Ray\3ds Max 2025\bin (Figure 5.13).
2. Select the Rendered Frames:
 – Browse to the folder where the EXR frames are saved.
 – Select the first EXR file, and V-Ray will process the entire sequence.

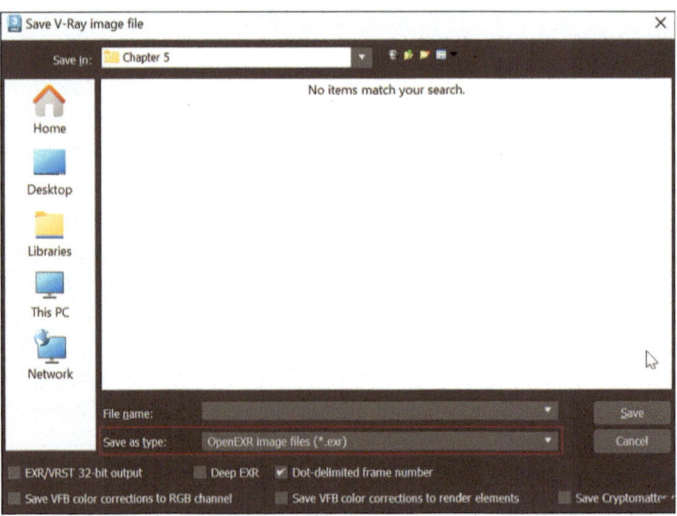

Figure 5.9

Choosing exr.

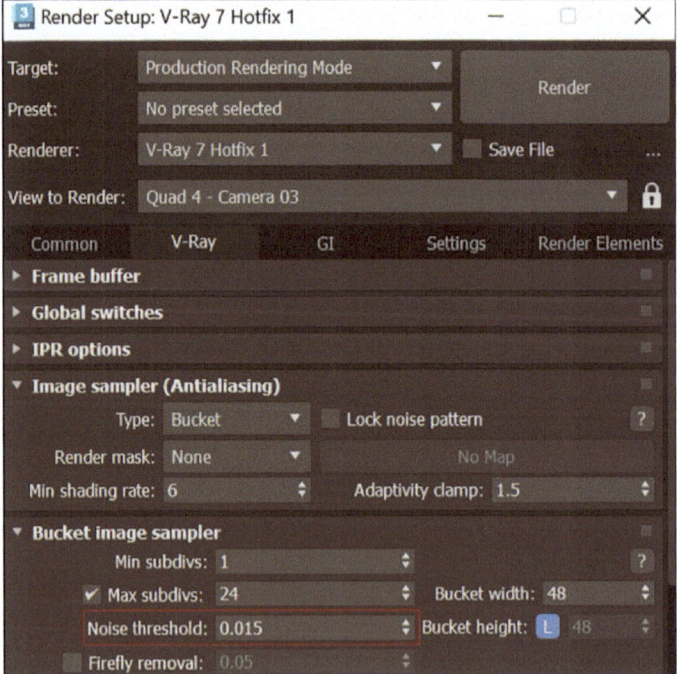

Figure 5.10

Setting the Noise threshold to 0.015.

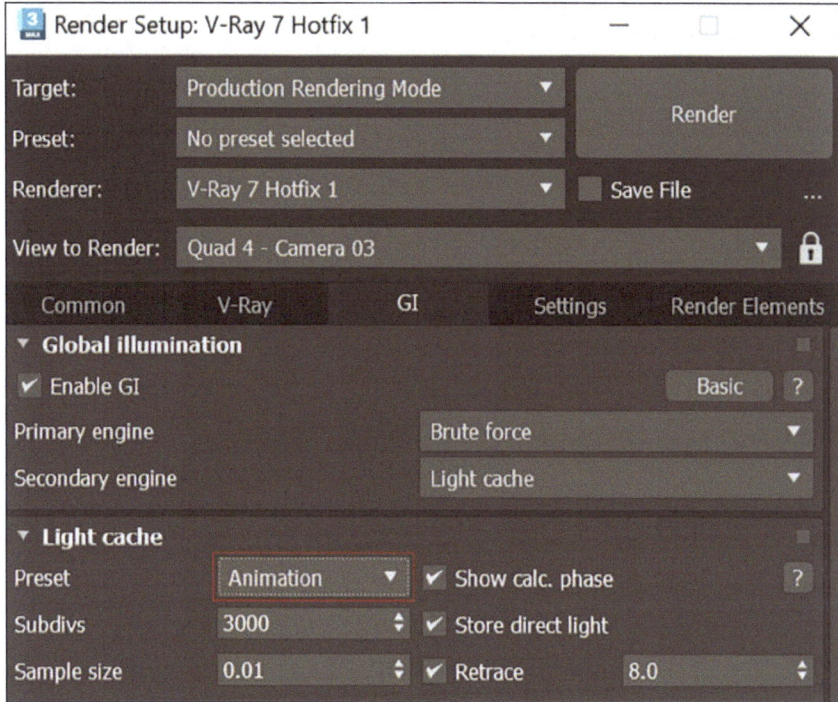

Figure 5.11

Setting Light Cache to Animation.

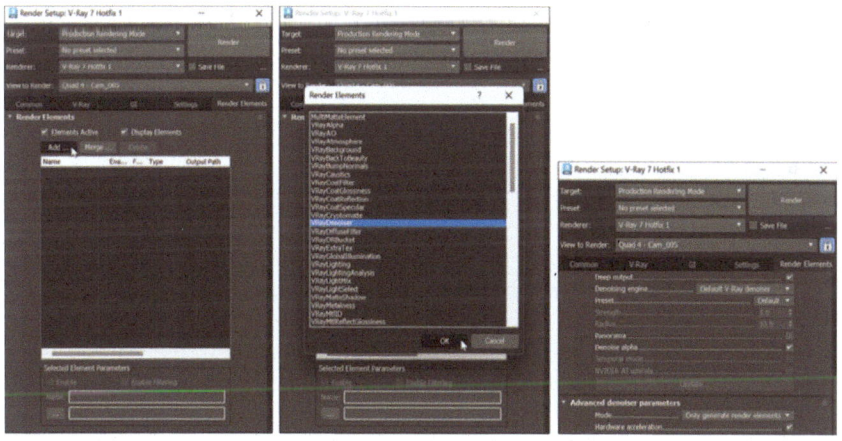

Figure 5.12

Adding the Denoiser Element.

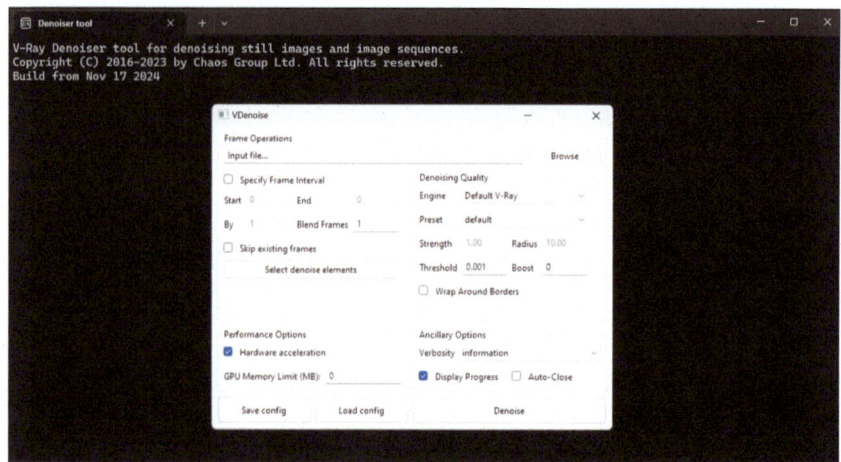

Figure 5.13

The Denoiser tool interface.

3. The tool will recognize the sequence and prompt for confirmation.
4. Select Render Elements for Denoising:
   – By default, only the RGB render element is denoised.
   – Additional elements can be selected using the Select denoise elements button (Figure 5.14).
5. Adjust the Denoising Settings, if necessary. Use the default options for the best results.
6. Click Denoise, and monitor the progress.
7. Save the Denoised EXR Files. The processed images will be saved in the original folder with a _denoised suffix.

5.4 Combining Images into a Movie

Once you have rendered all sequences, the final step is to combine them into a video. To do this, you need to use external software, such as Adobe After Effects or Adobe Premiere.

Step 1. Open the Software.

Step 2. Import Image Sequences.
   1. Load the Image Sequence:
      – In After Effects, go to File > Import > Multiple Files (Figure 5.16).

Ensure your images are numbered sequentially (i.e., frame_0001.png, frame_0002.png, etc.) so After Effects correctly identifies them as a sequence.

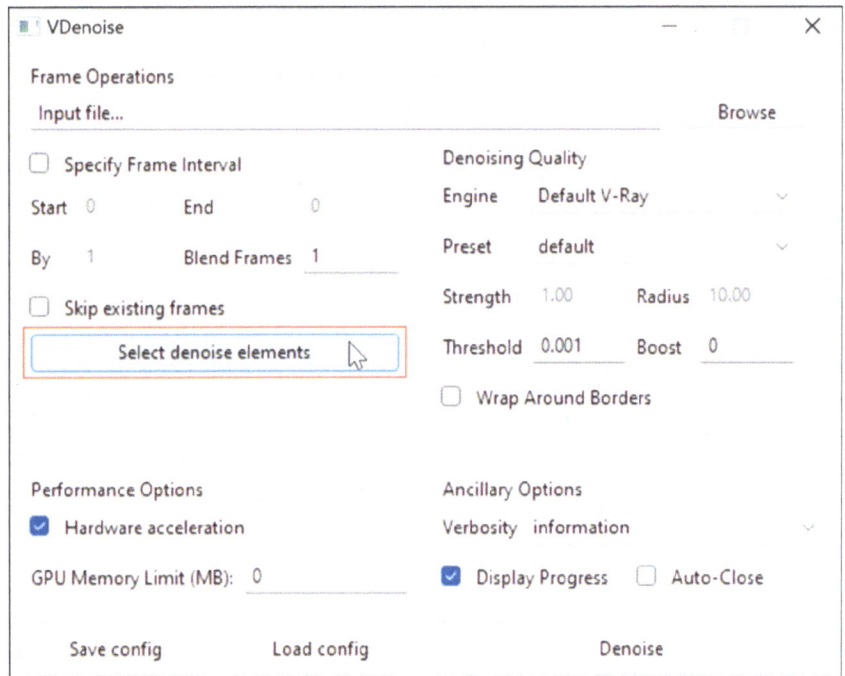

Figure 5.14

Clicking the Select denoise elements button.

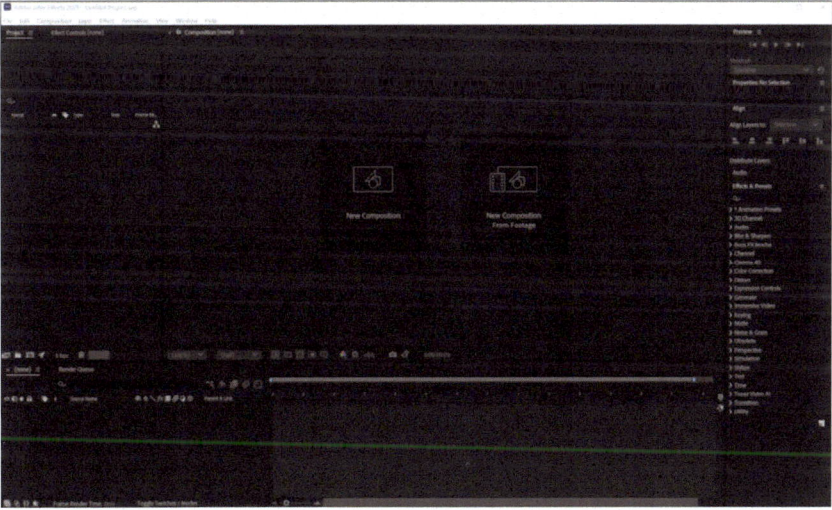

Figure 5.15

Adobe After Effects interface.

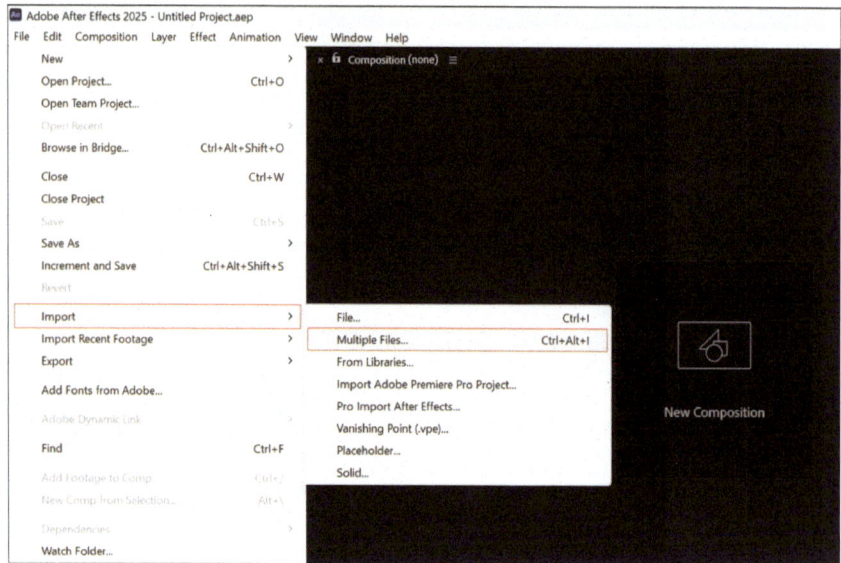

Figure 5.16

Choosing Multiple Files.

– Select the first image in the sequence, and click Import (Figure 5.17). The software will automatically detect and load the full sequence.
– When the Import Multiple Files dialog appears again, press Done to complete the process.

Step 3. Create a Composition.

1. Locate the imported image sequence in the Project Panel (left column).
2. Drag the sequence into the Composition Window at the bottom or onto the New Composition button (Figure 5.18).

Step 4. Preview the Animation.

– Press the Play button in the top-right corner to review your animation (Figure 5.19) (Video 5.1).
– Use the Timeline Scrubber to manually move through the frames, and ensure that all sequences are properly aligned.

Step 5. Export the Final Video.

1. Go to File > Export > Add to Render Queue.
2. In the Composition Window, click on the Output Module to adjust the settings (Figure 5.20). Choose the appropriate Format (H.264 for high quality and compatibility) (Figure 5.21).
3. Click on Output To to specify the file name, and save location (MP4 recommended) (Figure 5.22).
4. Click Render to begin exporting (Figure 5.23).

Step 6. Review the Final Output.

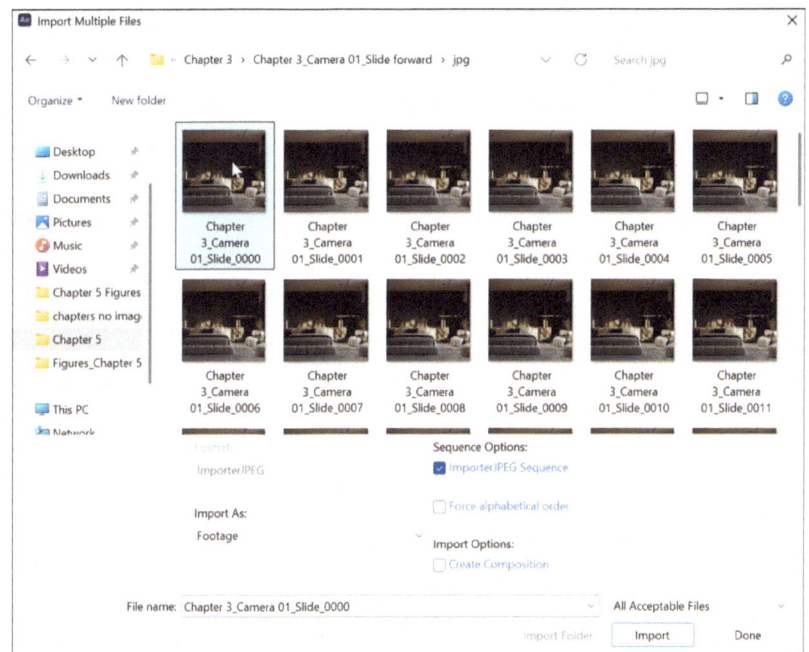

Selecting an image from the sequence and pressing Import.

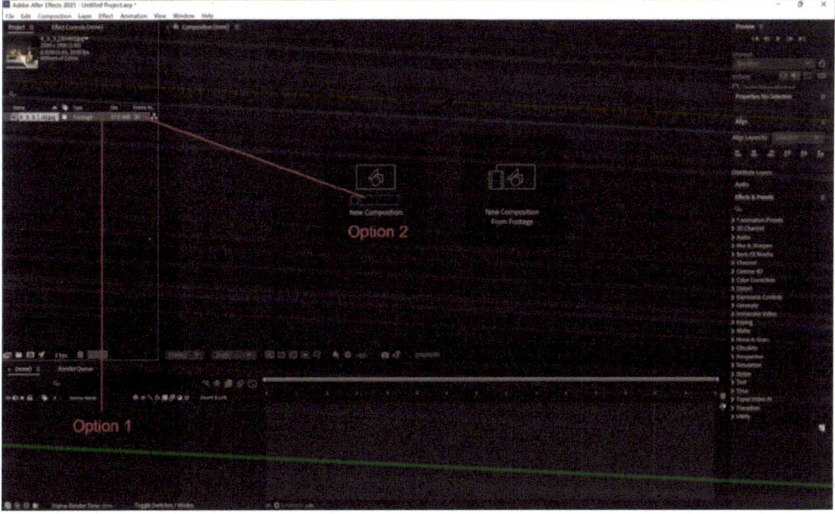

Dragging the Composition into the Composition Window (Option 1) or the New Composition button (Option 2).

Figure 5.19

Pressing the Play button to preview the animation.

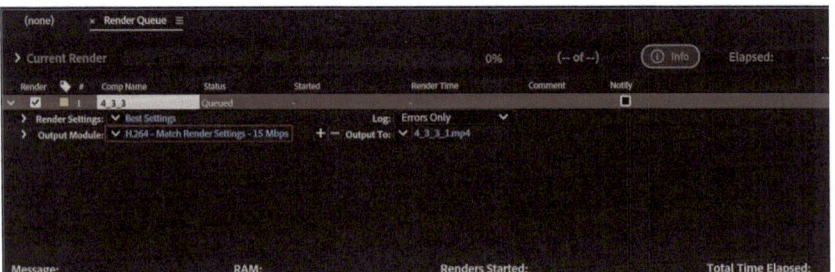

Figure 5.20

Clicking on the Output Module to adjust the settings.

Once the export is complete, open the video file in a media player to verify the quality. If necessary, adjust the settings and re-export for better results.

With these steps completed, your image sequence is now transformed into a smooth video animation.

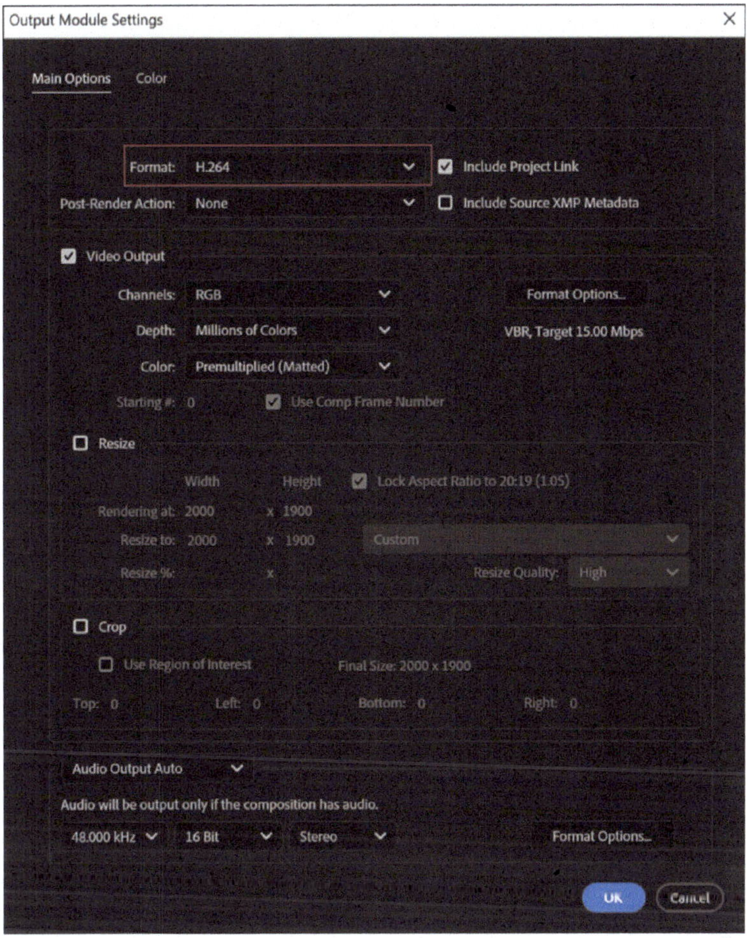

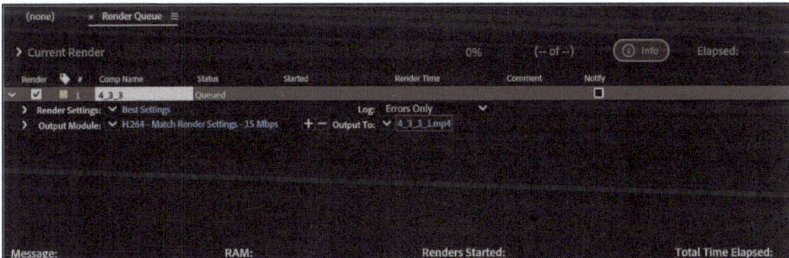

Figure 5.21

The Output Module Settings.

Figure 5.22

Clicking on the Output To to specify the file name and save location.

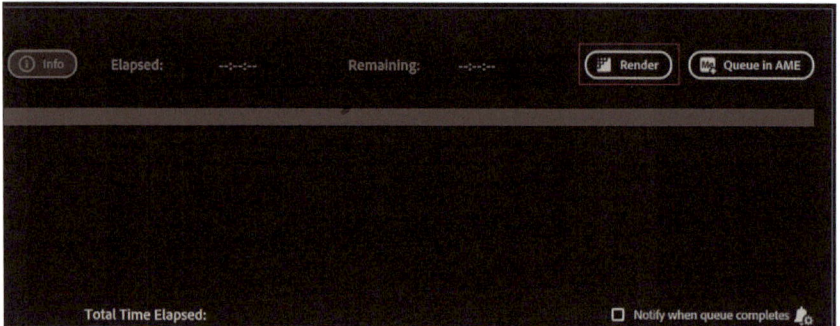

Figure 5.23

Clicking Render.

5.5 Rendering Using Chaos Cloud

If you are a V-Ray user, consider using Chaos Cloud to speed up your rendering process. Chaos Cloud is a cloud-based service that distributes your rendering workload across a network of powerful machines, freeing your local hardware for other tasks. Follow these steps to submit and manage your rendering job:

Step 1. Initiate the Submission.

In the V-Ray Toolbar, locate and click the Submit to Chaos Cloud rendering button (Figure 5.24).

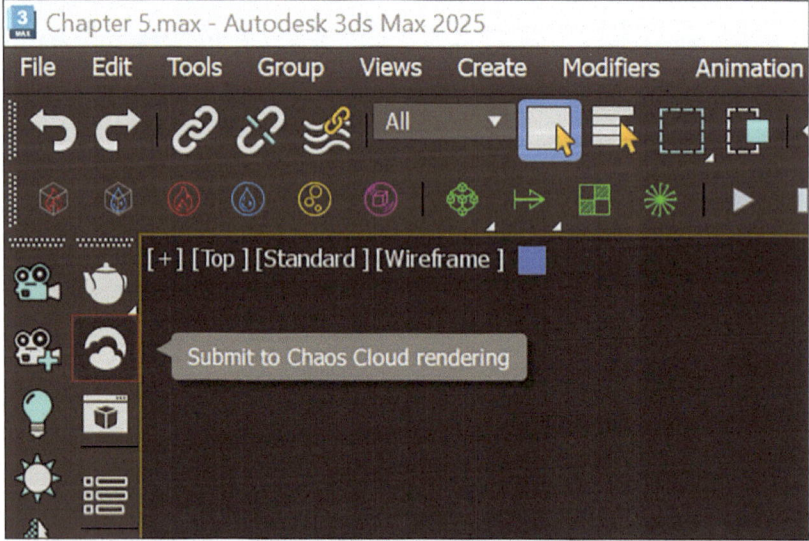

Figure 5.24

Clicking on the Submit to Chaos Cloud rendering button.

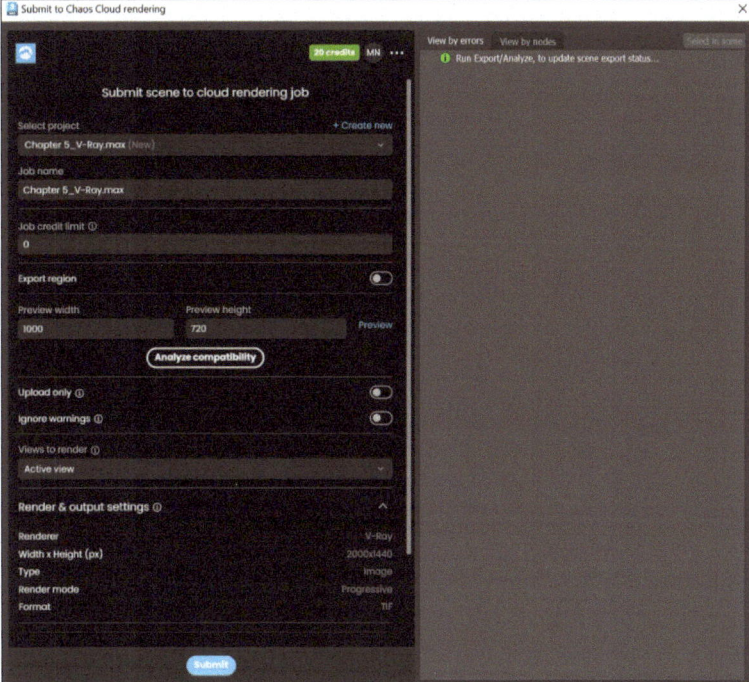

Figure 5.25

The Submit to Chaos Cloud rendering dialog.

Step 2. Configure Job Settings.

In the Submit to Chaos Cloud rendering dialog, review your project settings and press the Submit button (Figure 5.25). Your scene is now sent to Chaos Cloud, where it will be queued for rendering.

Step 3. Monitor Your Render.

Use the web interface to track your job's progress. This interface provides real-time updates and allows you to review individual frames as they render.

Step 4. Retrieve Your Render.

When rendering is complete, choose your preferred output:

- Preview MP4: A light, compressed video ideal for a quick review.
- Full EXR sequence: A high-quality sequence for detailed post-production work.

5.6 Topaz Labs

Topaz Labs offers AI-powered software that improves the quality of images and videos. In animation, this means you can render your work at a lower resolution to save time and resources, and then use Topaz to upscale your frames to a higher resolution.

Key products include:

- **Topaz Gigapixel AI:**
  Enhances still images by adding details, sharpening edges, and reducing noise.
- **Topaz Video AI:**
  Processes video frames to create smooth, high-resolution results.

Using these tools lets animators save time and reduce costs, as high-resolution rendering can be very demanding. By adding Topaz Labs to your workflow, you can efficiently create high-quality visuals and explore creative options by starting with low-resolution renders that are later transformed into high-resolution animations.

5.6.1 Step-by-Step Example: Using Topaz Video AI to Upscale a Video

Step 1. Render Low-Resolution Animation.

Begin by rendering your animation at a lower resolution to save time and computing resources.

Step 2. Import Your Video in Topaz Video AI.
1. Open Topaz Video AI (Figure 5.26).
2. Load your animation into the software by dragging and dropping the file or by clicking the Browse Videos button (Figure 5.27).

Step 3. Select a Preset.
1. A pop-up window appears with your animation in the background and preset options on the right.
2. Choose a preset, for example, to Upscale to 4K (see Figure 5.28).

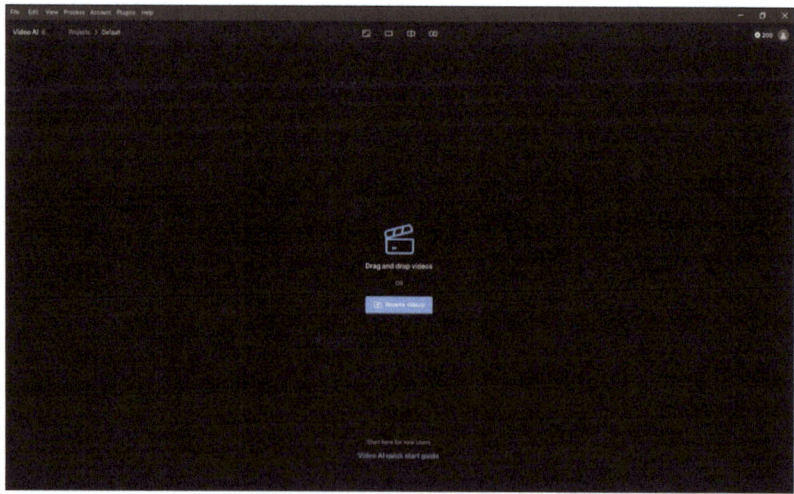

Figure 5.26

The Topaz Video AI interface.

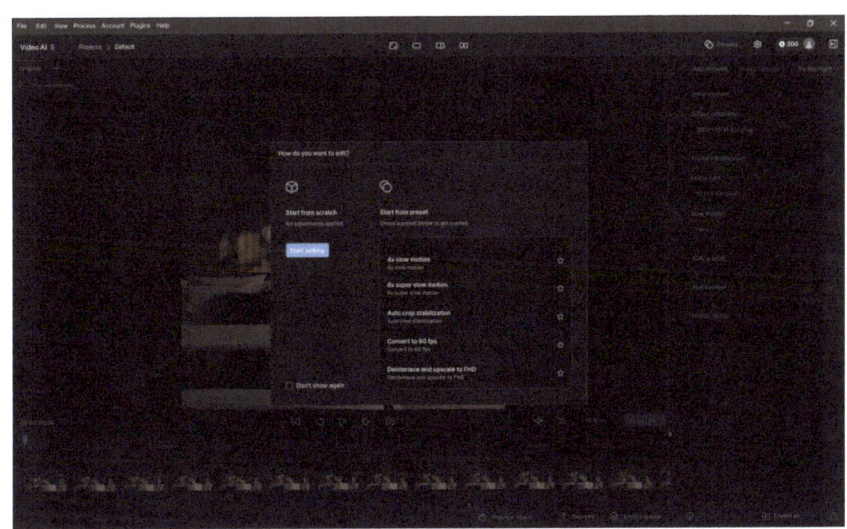

Figure 5.27

The Topaz Video AI interface.

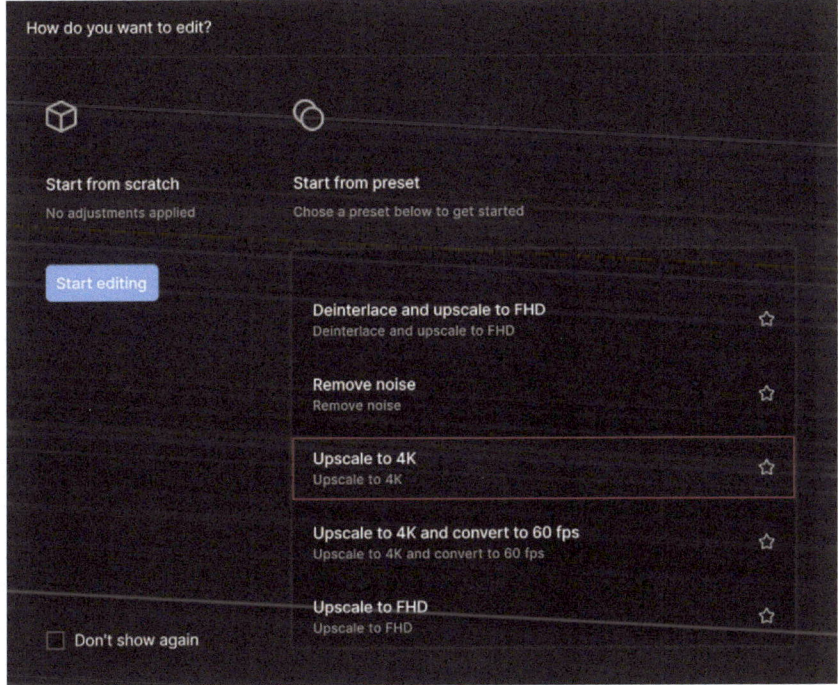

Figure 5.28

Selecting to Upscale to 4K.

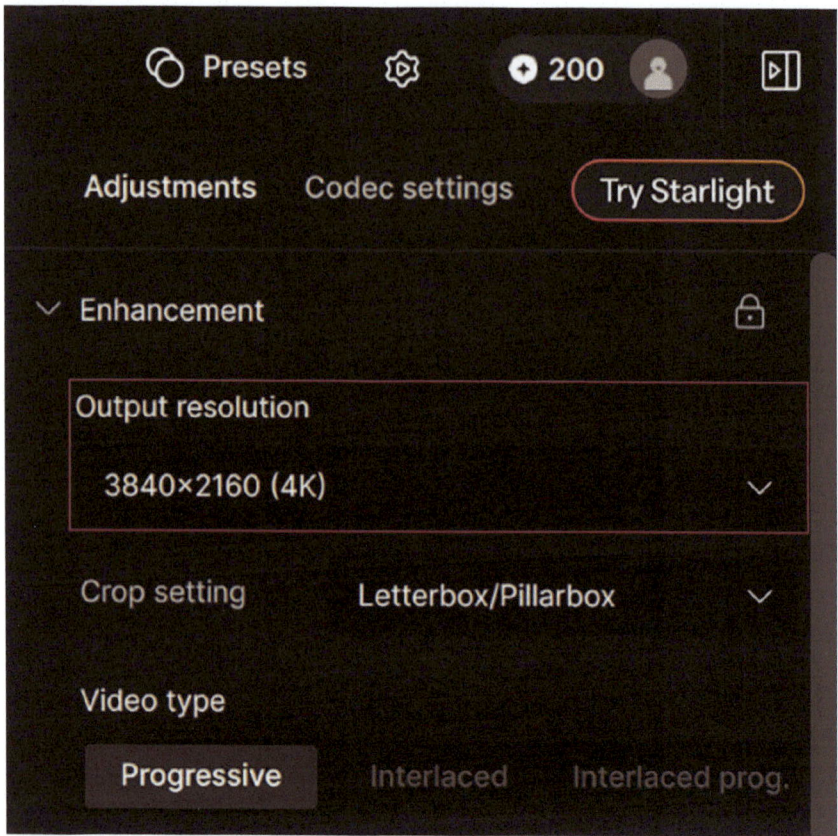

Figure 5.29

Checking the Output resolution.

Step 4. Set the Output Resolution.
- In the Enhancement section, check the Output Resolution field, and you see that the video is converted to 3,840×2,160 (4K) (Figure 5.29).
- If desired, change this by selecting another preset or choose Custom Resolution to enter your preferred dimensions.

Step 5. Choose the AI Model (Figure 5.30).

Step 6. Preview the Enhancement.

Use the side-by-side comparison at the top of the interface, to see the original on the left and the enhanced version on the right (Figure 5.31).

Step 7. Test the Settings.

Click the Render 2s button to process a short segment of the video, and review the effect of your chosen settings (Figure 5.32).

Step 8. Export the Enhanced Video.

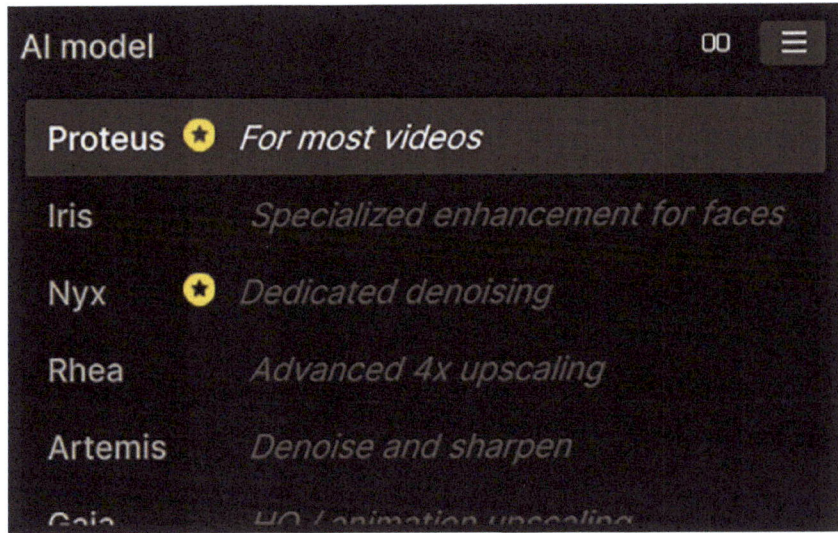

Figure 5.30

Choosing an AI model.

Figure 5.31

Choosing the side-by-side comparison.

Click the Quick Export button (Figure 5.33). The software will export the enhanced video to the same location as the input file, using a matching file name.

Figure 5.33

Exporting the animation.

By following these steps, you can efficiently transform low-resolution renders into high-quality animations using Topaz Video AI.

5.6.2 Step-by-Step Example: Using Topaz Video AI to Combine Images into a Video

Instead of using Adobe After Effects, you can use Topaz to combine the renders into a video.

Step 1. Import Your Sequence in Topaz Video AI.

1. Open Topaz Video AI.
2. Click on the Browse Videos button.

3. In the Open dialog, click on Video files and choose Image sequences (Figure 5.34).
4. Select the first image of the sequence, and press Open (Figure 5.35).

Step 2. Preview the Animation.

Press the Play button to preview the animation.

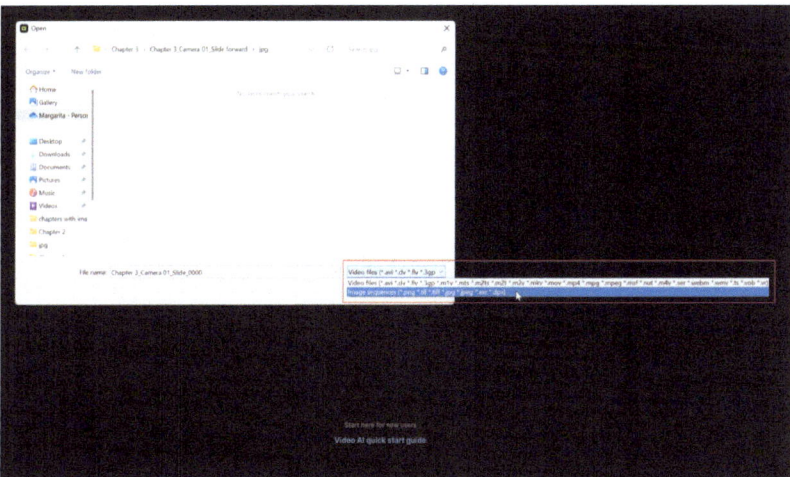

Figure 5.34

Choosing Image sequences.

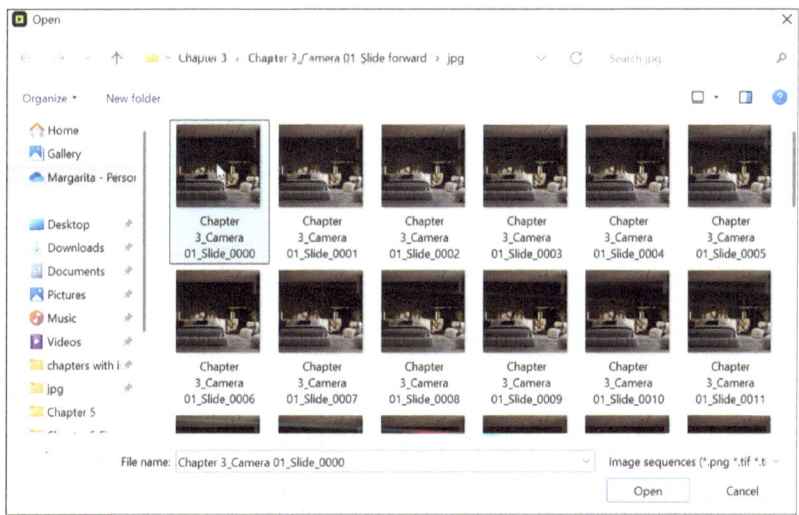

Figure 5.35

Selecting the first image of the sequence.

Figure 5.36

Pressing Play to preview the animation.

5.6.3 Step-by-Step Example: Using Topaz Video AI for Frame Interpolation

Another useful feature of Topaz Video AI is frame interpolation. It allows you to increase the frame rate of your animation by generating new frames between existing ones, making the motion smoother. If used for slow-motion effects, it can also extend the duration of your animation without making it look choppy.

Step 1. Import Your Sequence in Topaz Video AI.

1. Open Topaz Video AI.
2. Import your sequence or animation.

Step 2. Select Frame Interpolation Mode.

1. Toggle Frame Interpolation to ON (Figure 5.37).
2. Choose the AI model:
   - Apollo: Best for general motion interpolation.
   - Chronos: Best for creating smooth slow-motion effects.
   - Chronos Fast: A faster version of Chronos with slightly less accuracy.
     For this example, let's select Chronos for high-quality interpolation (Figure 5.38).
3. Choose the Slow motion model.
   Set the speed factor, i.e., 2x for half-speed (Figure 5.39).

Step 3. Export the Final Video.

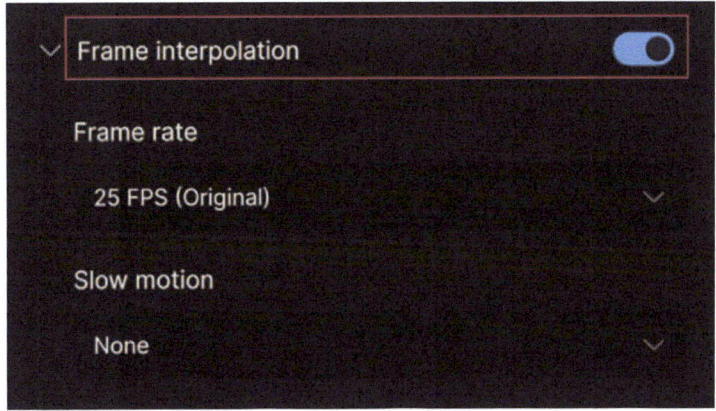

Figure 5.37

Enabling Frame Interpolation.

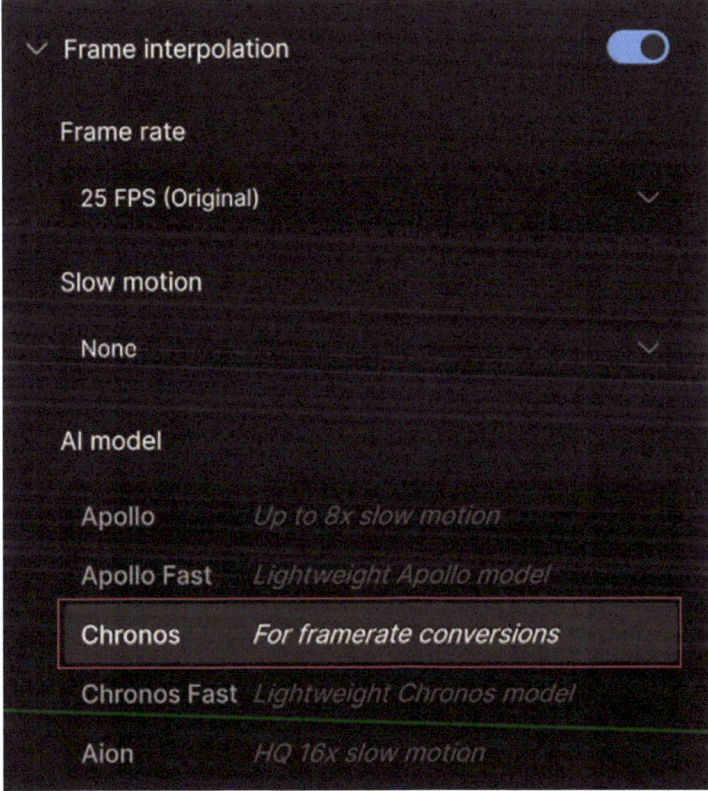

Figure 5.38

Choosing Chronos.

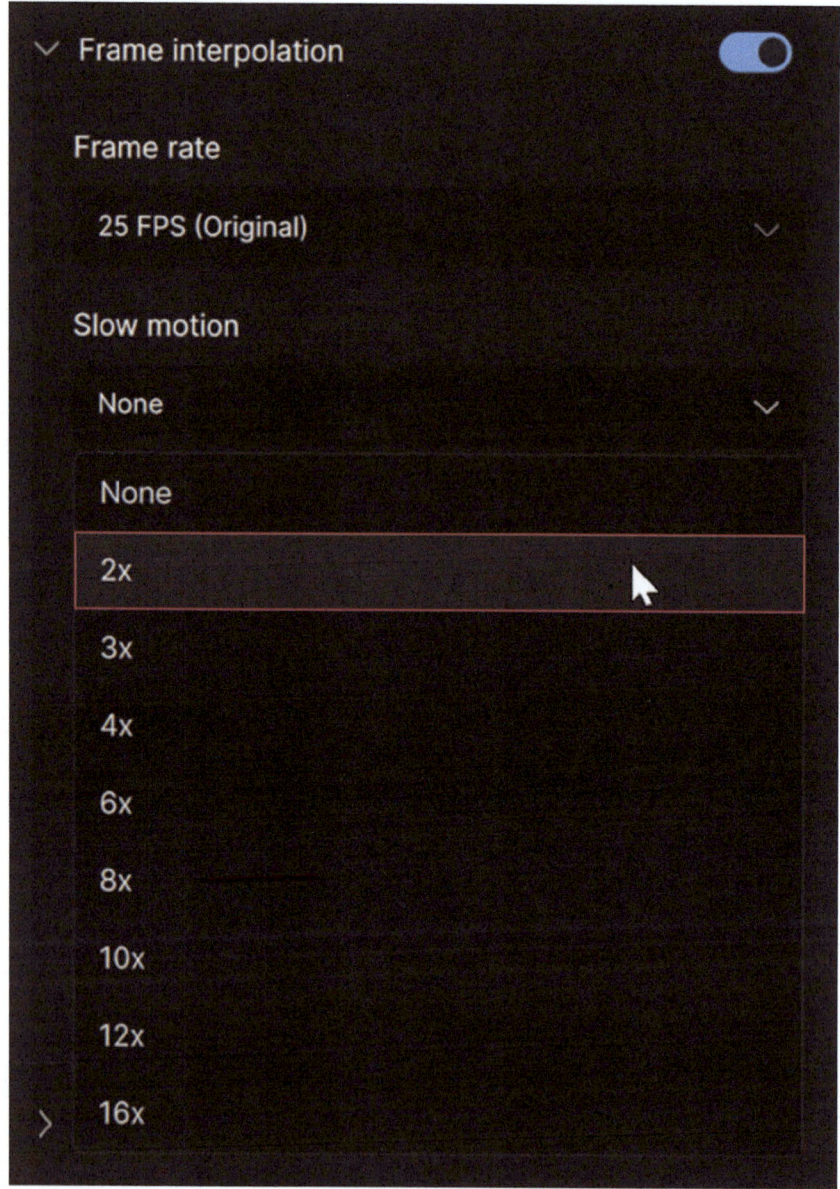

Figure 5.39

Slowing motion 2x.

By using Topaz Video AI's frame interpolation, you can dramatically improve the smoothness of your animation, whether you are increasing the frame rate for realism or creating high-quality slow-motion effects.

6

Simulations

6.1 Installing Chaos Phoenix

Before you start simulations, you need to install Chaos Phoenix. If you already have an active license for Corona or V-Ray, follow these steps to download and install PhoenixFD:

1. Navigate to my.chaos.com/products.
2. In the Download menu, click on All Products.
3. Locate Phoenix for 3ds Max in the list.
4. Select the appropriate Platform version for your setup.
5. Click Download (Figure 6.1).

Once the download is complete, run the installer and follow the on-screen instructions to integrate Phoenix into your 3ds Max environment. In Figure 6.2, you see the PhoenixFD Toolbar. Dock it, and you are ready to dive into the world of simulations!

DOI: 10.1201/9781003651222-6

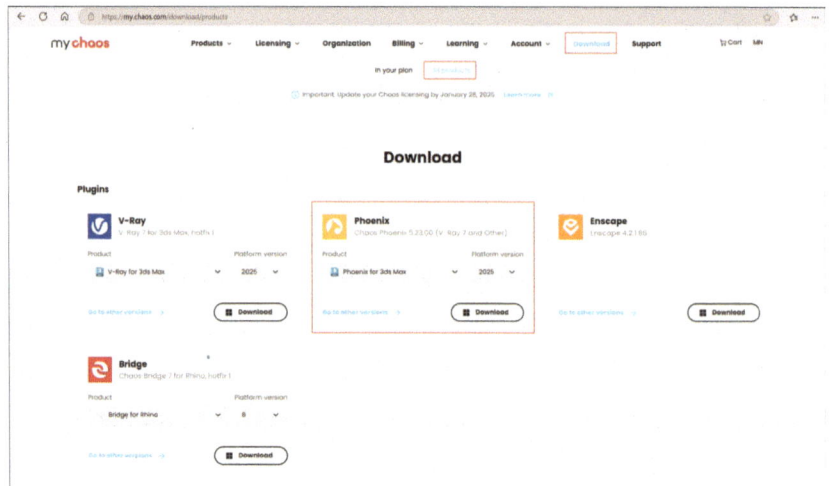

Figure 6.1

Screenshot of the mychaos website showcasing the steps to download Phoenix for 3ds Max.

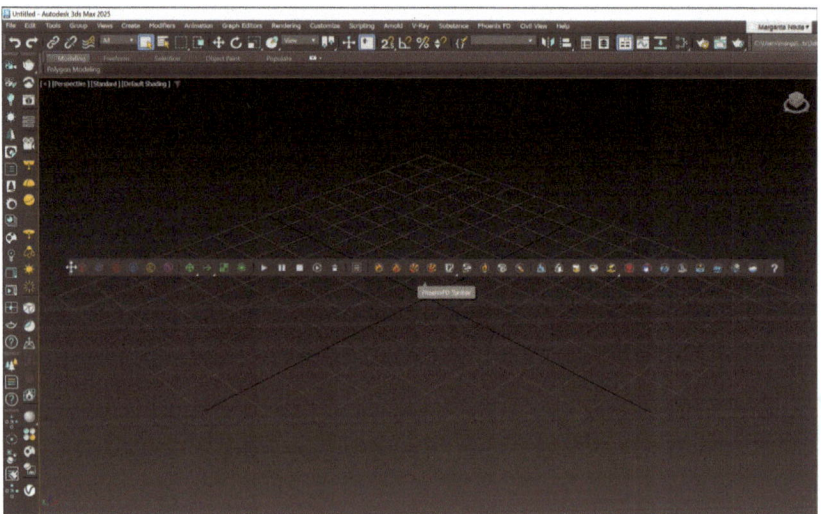

Figure 6.2

The Chaos Phoenix toolbar floating in the viewport.

6.2 Water Faucet Simulation

To get started, open the file Chapter 6.max. In the Camera 01 viewport, you see a close-up view of the bar faucet. In this section, you will learn how to create a realistic water flow from the faucet using Chaos Phoenix.

Figure 6.3

The PhoenixFD Toolbar docked.

Figure 6.4

Rendered image of the faucet before applying the water simulation.

This process involves setting up a water simulation, adjusting the parameters for realistic movement, and rendering the final scene with lifelike materials.

If you render the scene at this stage, you will get the result shown in Figure 6.4.

6.2.1 Step-by-Step Example: Faucet Water Simulation

Step 1. Isolate and Prepare the Faucet for Simulation.

1. Select the faucet by clicking on it.
2. Right-click and choose Isolate Selection (Figure 6.5). Isolating the faucet makes it easier to focus on creating and adjusting the water flow without distractions from other elements in the scene.
3. Switch to a Perspective view, and rotate the viewport to see the interior of the faucet where the water will flow (Figure 6.6). This ensures

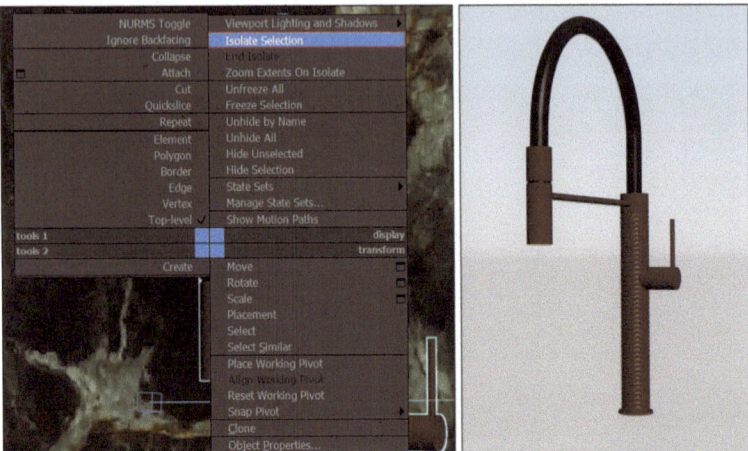

Figure 6.5

Isolating the faucet using the right-click menu.

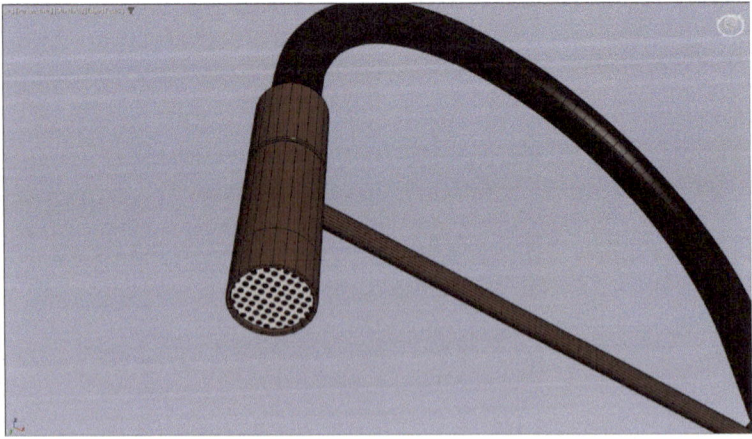

Figure 6.6

Perspective viewport showing the interior of the faucet.

that you are aware of the internal structure, which is critical for placing the water source.

4. With the faucet selected, go to the Modify panel, navigate to the Selection rollout, and choose Edge (Figure 6.7).
5. Enable Edged Faces in the viewport to make the faucet's edges visible (Figure 6.8).

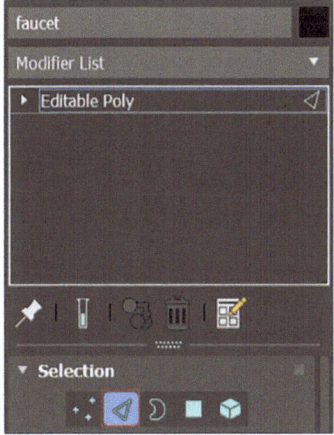

Figure 6.7

Enabling the Edge selection in the Modify panel.

Figure 6.8

Enabling Edged Faces in the Perspective viewport.

Step 2. Create the Water Path.

1. Click on an edge inside the faucet's opening, as shown in Figure 6.9.
2. Use the Loop command to select all connected edges (Figure 6.10). This step identifies the full perimeter of the faucet's opening.
3. Click Create Shape From Selection, select Linear in the dialog box, and press OK (Figure 6.11). This creates a shape to guide the water flow.
4. Disable the Edge selection in the Modify panel to exit the edge editing mode and continue modifying the object as a whole.

Step 3. Adjust the Shape's Pivot.

1. Select the newly created shape, Shape001.
2. Go to the Hierarchy tab, and under Adjust Pivot, click Affect Pivot Only. Then, click Center to Object (Figure 6.12). This centers the pivot for easier transformations.
3. Disable the Affect Pivot Only mode.

Step 4. Convert the Shape to an Editable Poly.

1. With the shape selected, add an Edit Poly modifier from the Modifier list (Figure 6.13).
2. In the Utilities panel, click More, select UVW Remove, and click Materials to clear the existing materials (Figure 6.14).

Step 5. Set Up the Water Simulation.

1. Go to the PhoenixFD Toolbar.
2. Click Setup a Tap Water sim for the selected objects (Figure 6.15).
   - A wireframe box appears representing the simulation area (Figure 6.16).

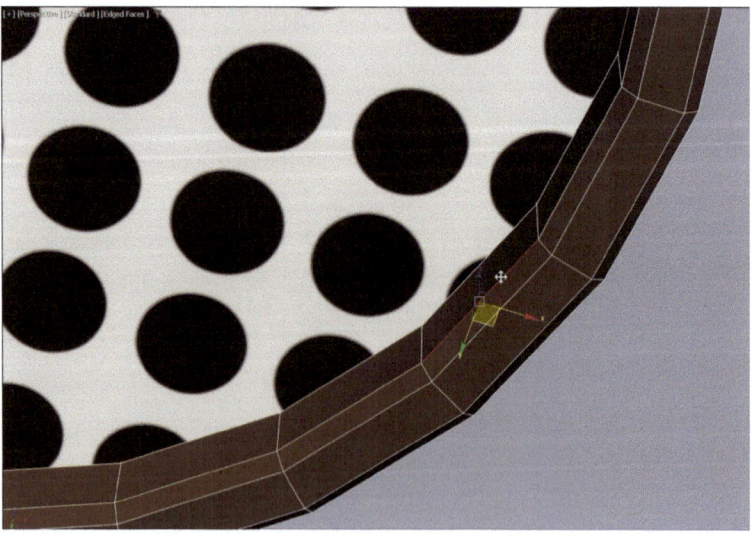

Figure 6.9

Selecting an edge on the faucet.

Figure 6.10

Using the Loop command to select connected edges.

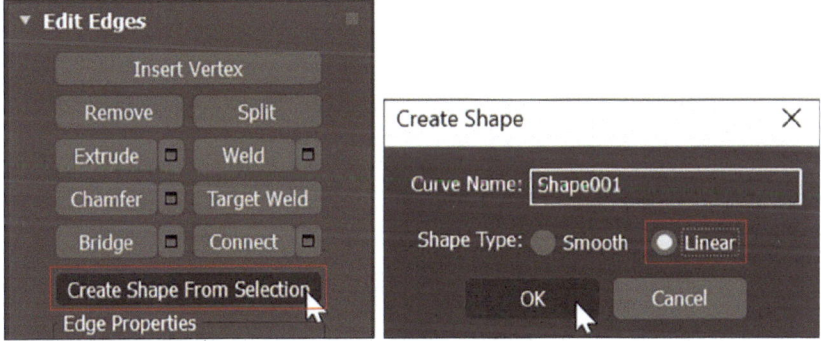

Figure 6.11

Creating a shape from the selected edges.

> – Adjust the size of the grid/wireframe box to fit the scene, as the water will interact with the sink.

3. Exit Isolate Mode and isolate the relevant objects: the faucet, the bar sink, Shape001, LiquidSrc001, and PhoenixFDLiquid001 (Figure 6.18).

4. Adjust the PhoenixFDLiquid001 position to touch the sink base (Figure 6.19). Positioning the liquid source correctly ensures that water flows naturally into the sink.

Figure 6.12

Centering the shape's pivot.

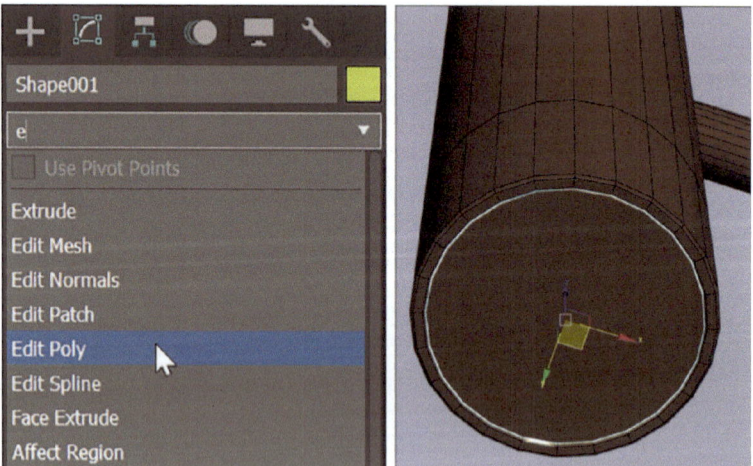

Figure 6.13

Adding the Edit Poly Modifier.

5. In the Modify panel, go to the Grid rollout and resize the grid to include the faucet. A larger grid accommodates splashes and ensures realistic behavior (Figure 6.20).

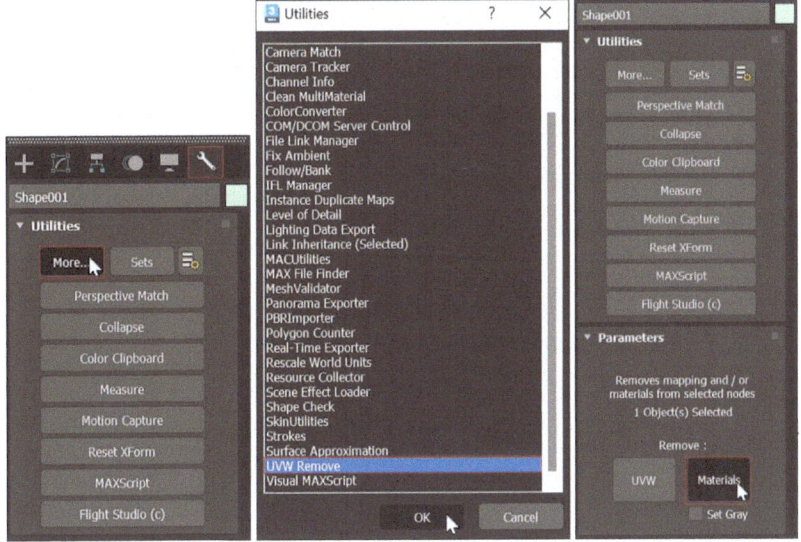

Figure 6.14

Steps to remove the materials from the shape.

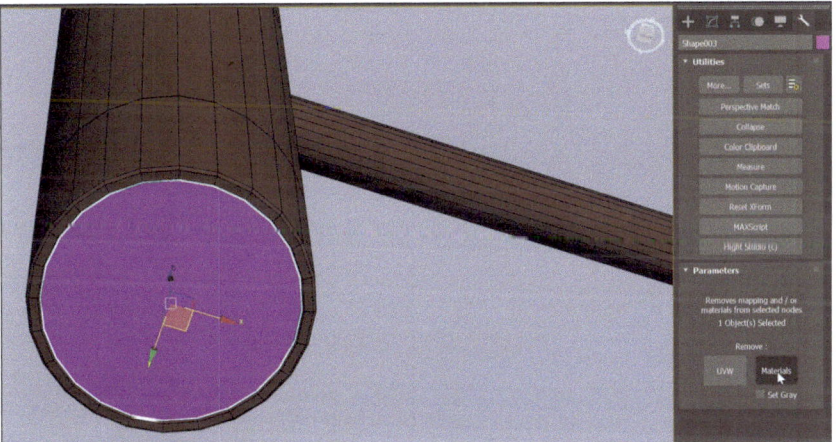

Figure 6.15

Material removed from the shape.

6. Optimize performance by setting the Scene Scale to 1 and increasing the voxel size (Figure 6.21). Larger voxels speed up the simulation at the expense of detail. For this example, change the voxel size from 0.054 to 0.065 cm.

7. In the Dynamics rollout, set 10 Steps per Frame to refine the simulation's accuracy (Figure 6.22).

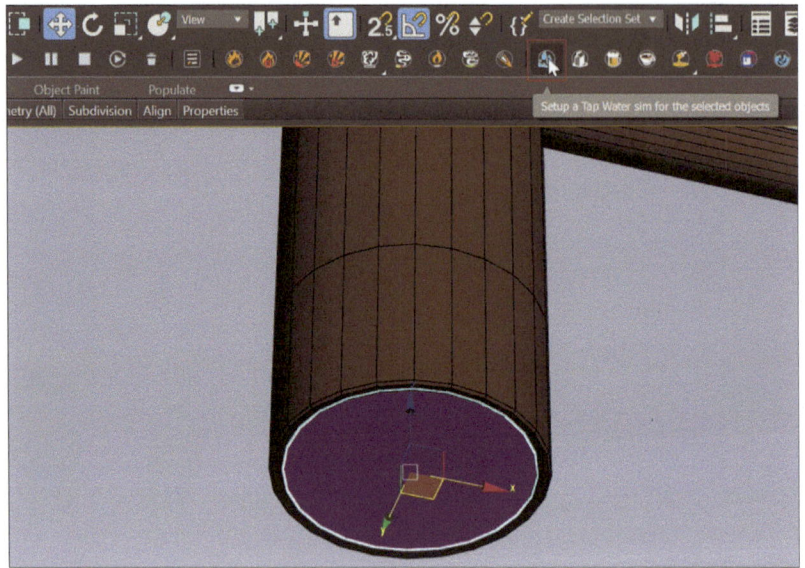

Figure 6.16

The Setup a Tap Water sim for the selected objects in the PhoenixFD Toolbar.

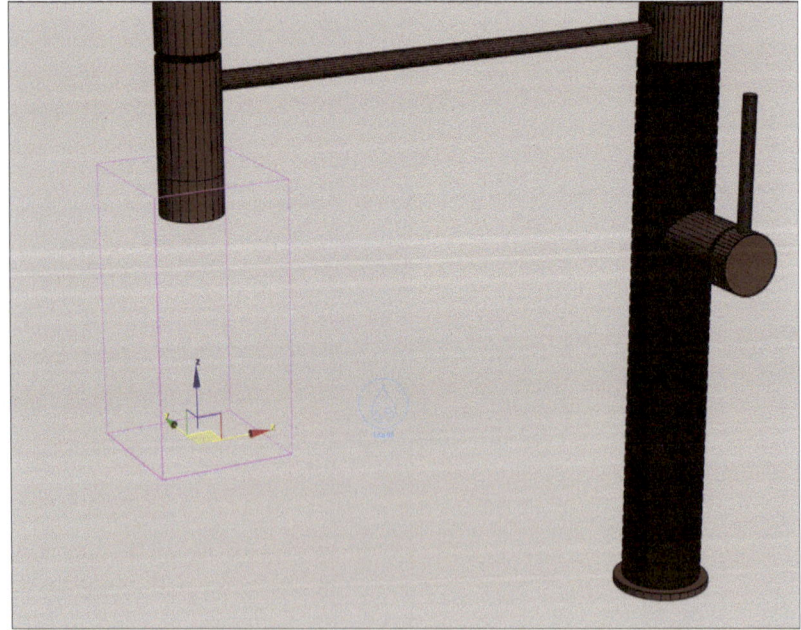

Figure 6.17

The wireframe box representing the simulation area.

Figure 6.18
Isolating the necessary components.

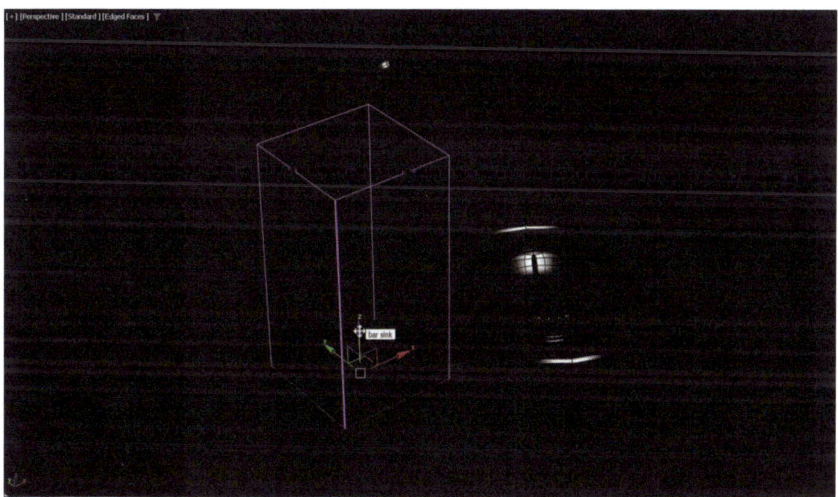

Figure 6.19
Adjusting the simulation grid position.

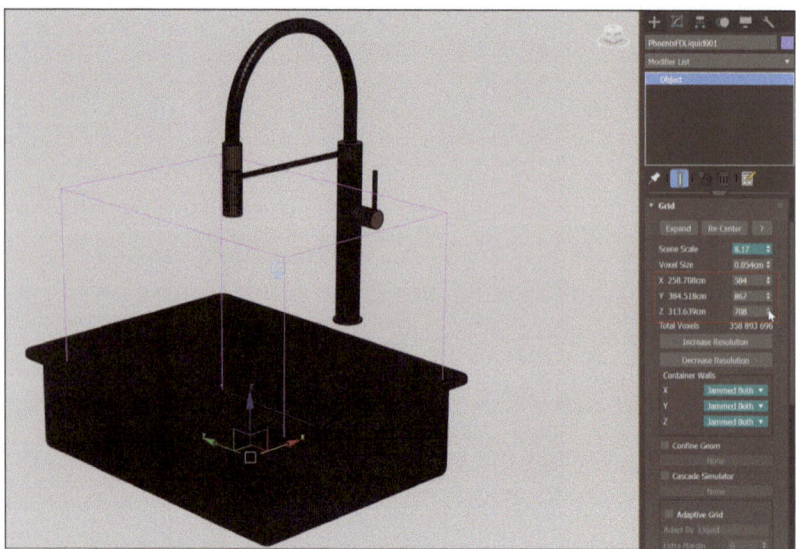

Figure 6.20

Adjusting the Grid size.

8. Disable Show Particle Preview, in the Preview rollout to reduce GPU load (Figure 6.23).

Step 6. Fine-Tune the Simulation.

1. Select the liquid icon. Go to the Outgoing Velocity to control water pressure. For example, increasing velocity from 2.596 to 100 cm will make the flow stronger (Figure 6.24).

2. Start the simulation by clicking Start in the Simulation rollout (Figure 6.25), or from the PhoenixFD Toolbar.

3. View the simulation results at different frames, i.e., at Frames 9 and 16 in Figure 6.26.

Step 7. Making Changes to the Water Simulation.

1. To make any changes, stop the simulation by pressing either the Stop button at the PhoenixFD Toolbar or the Stop button in the Simulation rollout (Figure 6.27).

2. Additionally, make sure to click on the Delete the Phoenix Simulation Cache Files button (Figure 6.28). This step is important because it clears any previously generated simulation data, ensuring that your new simulation runs from scratch with the updated settings. Without deleting the cache files, 3ds Max might use old data, which can cause unexpected results or prevent changes from appearing correctly in your simulation.

3. Select the liquid icon, change the velocity to 20 cm and start a new simulation (Figure 6.29).

Figure 6.21

Adjusting the Scene Scale and Voxel Size settings.

Step 8. Apply a Material to the Water.
1. Open the Material Editor (press M), and create a CoronaPhysicalMtl.
2. From the Preset list, select Water and apply it to the simulated liquid (Figure 6.30).

Step 9. Render the Final Output.
1. Shape001 can be removed after the simulation. Either delete it or hide it. This is because Shape001 is only used as a reference or helper object during the simulation setup. Once the simulation is complete, it no longer affects the final result.
2. End the isolation mode.
3. Switch to Camera 01 viewport.

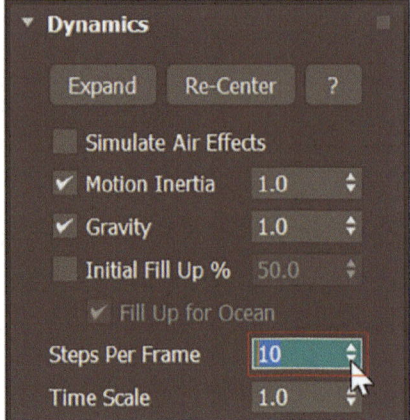

Figure 6.22

Optimizing the Dynamics settings.

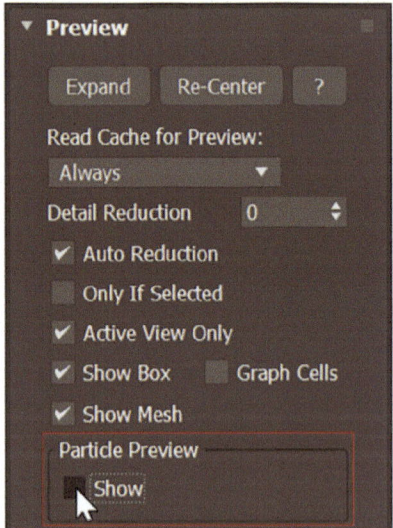

Figure 6.23

Disabling the Particle Preview.

4. Choose a frame, i.e., Frame 60, and produce a render to view how the water looks (Figure 6.31).
5. For a smoother appearance, go to Mesh Smoothing in the Rendering rollout, and set it to 2 (Figures 6.32).
6. Set an additional camera to see the interior of the sink for an alternative view and produce a render (Figure 6.33).

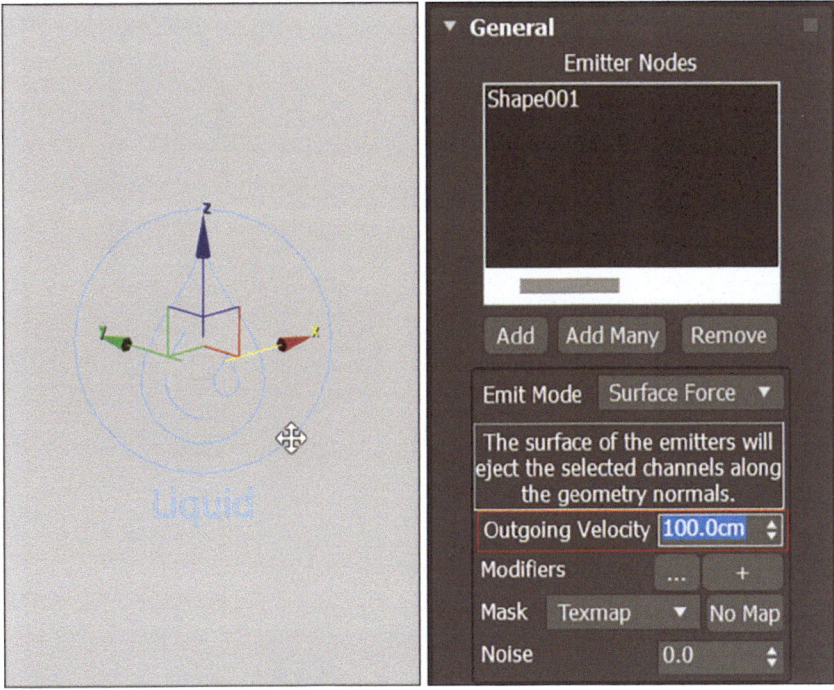

Figure 6.24

Adjusting the Outgoing Velocity.

Figure 6.25

Starting the water simulation.

Figure 6.26

Water simulation at Frames 9 and 16.

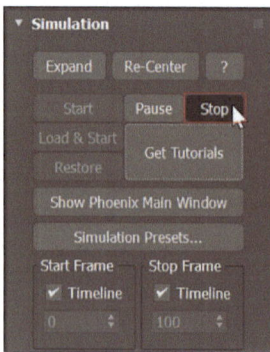

Figure 6.27

Ways to stop the simulation.

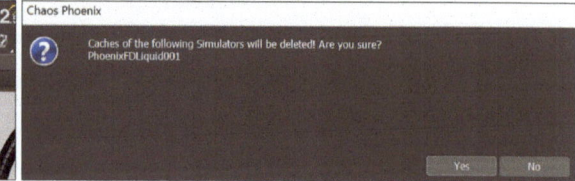

Figure 6.28

Deleting the cache files.

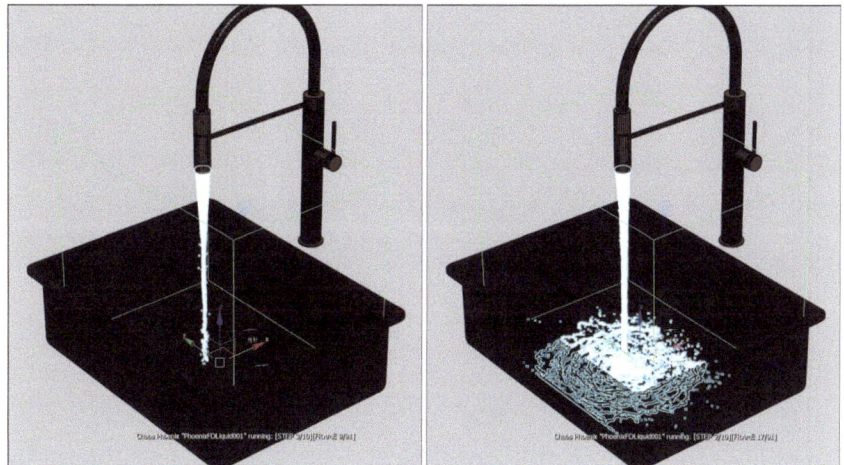

Figure 6.29

Screenshots of the new simulation at Frames 9 and 17 with adjusted Outgoing Velocity at 20 cm.

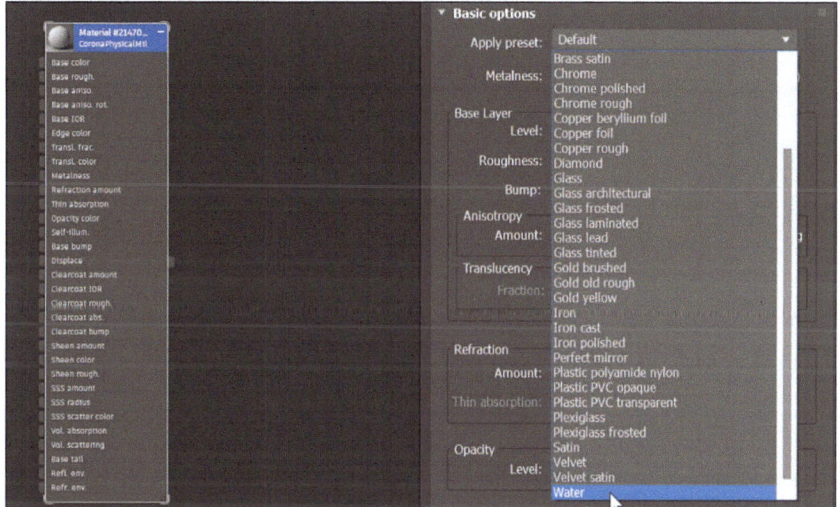

Figure 6.30

Applying the Water preset.

In this section, you learned how to simulate a realistic water flow from a faucet using Chaos Phoenix. By isolating the faucet, defining the flow path, setting up the simulation parameters, and applying appropriate materials, you created a photorealistic scene that captures the dynamic behavior of water. By experimenting

Render of the water simulation at Frame 60.

with different settings, you can customize the simulation to fit various scenarios, expanding your skills in creating compelling animations for diverse projects.

6.3 Fireplace Simulation

In this section, you will learn how to create a realistic fireplace fire using Chaos Phoenix. To begin, go to Camera 03 viewport, which provides a close-up view of the fireplace (Figure 6.34).

The scene features a modern bio-ethanol fireplace with a dedicated fire chamber. If you render the scene at this stage, you will get the image of Figure 6.35.

By the end of this section, you will have created a dynamic and visually convincing fire simulation that integrates naturally within the scene.

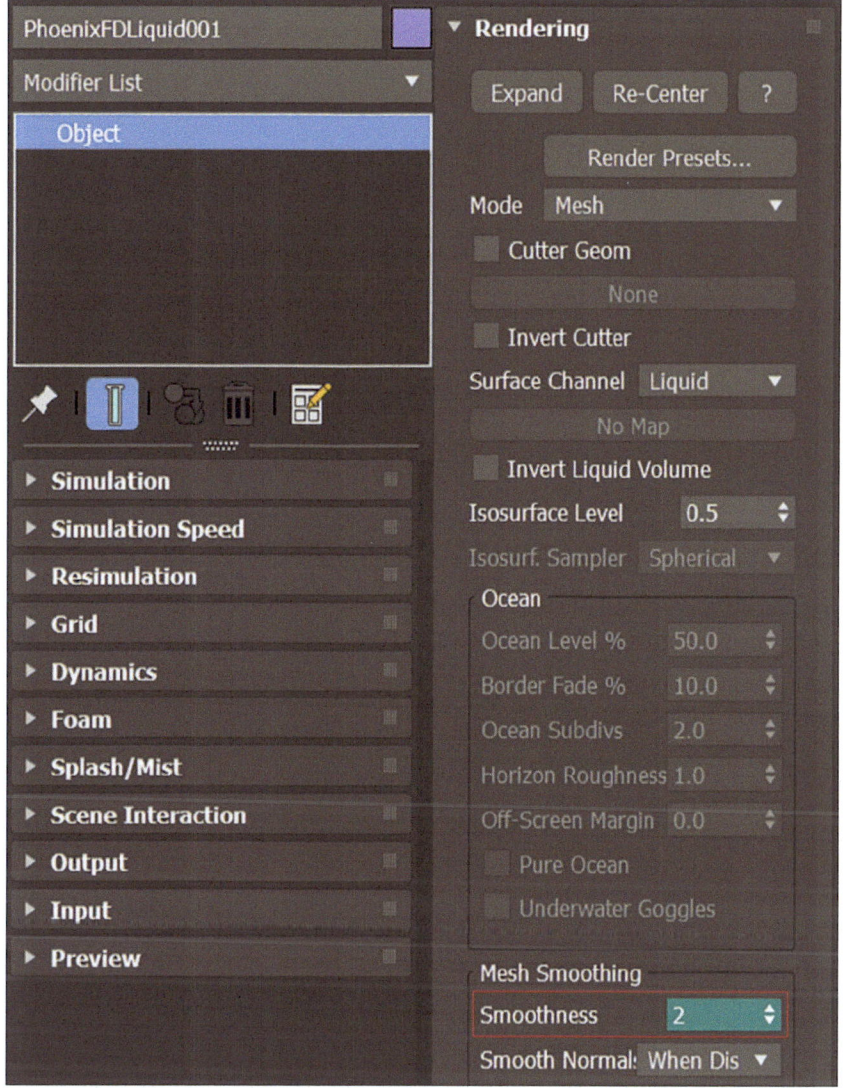

Figure 6.32

Setting Smoothness to 2.

6.3.1 Step-by-Step Example: Fireplace Fire Simulation

Step 1. Create the Combustion Source.

To simulate fire, you need a source to initiate combustion. In this case, you need to create a simple box inside the fireplace chamber.

1. Select the fireplace metal object, right-click, and choose Isolate Selection.

Figure 6.33

Render of the new camera.

2. Switch to a Perspective view to work more easily.
3. Create the combustion box:
   - Create a box, and position it inside the metal chamber.
   - Ensure that its dimensions align with the chamber's size (Figure 6.36).

Step 2. Create the Fire Simulation Container.
1. With the box selected, go to the PhoenixFD Toolbar, and click Set up Fire Sim (Figure 6.37). This creates a simulation container using a fire preset (Figure 6.38).
2. Click Time Configuration, and set the FPS to 30 and the Length to 300 Frames (Figure 6.39 – left).
3. Start the simulation by clicking the Start Simulation button from the PhoenixFD Toolbar (Figure 6.40 – right) (Video 6.1).
   Observations:

Figure 6.34

Screenshot of Camera 03 viewport.

At this stage, the flame may appear small and move too quickly. The next step is to adjust the simulation to achieve a more realistic result.

Step 3. Adjust the Fire's Size.
1. Delete the existing cache files by pressing Delete the Phoenix Simulation Cache Files (Figure 6.40).
2. Drag the Time Slider back to Frame 0.
3. Adjust the simulation grid size:
    - Go to the Grid rollout in the Modify panel, and modify the X, Y, and Z values to fit the desired size of the flames (Figure 6.41).
4. Increase the Scene Scale to 10 to enlarge the flames. The larger this value, the larger the flames (Figure 6.42).
5. Start a new simulation (Figure 6.43 and Video 6.2).

Step 4. Adjust the Fire's Speed.
1. Delete the cache files, and reset the Timeline to Frame 0.

Figure 6.35

Render from Camera 03.

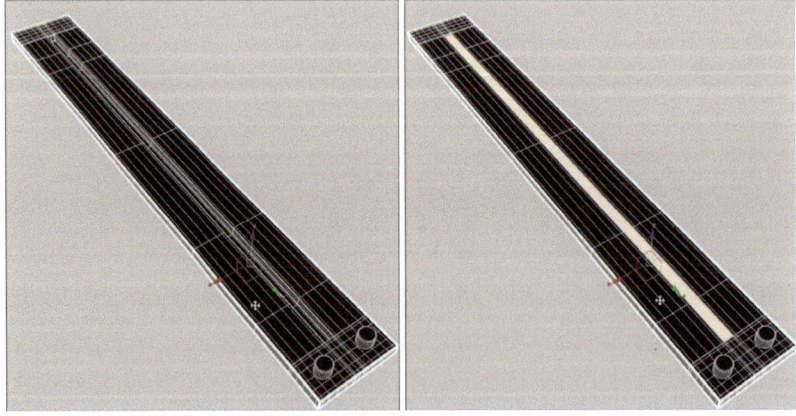

Figure 6.36

Box placed in the fireplace chamber.

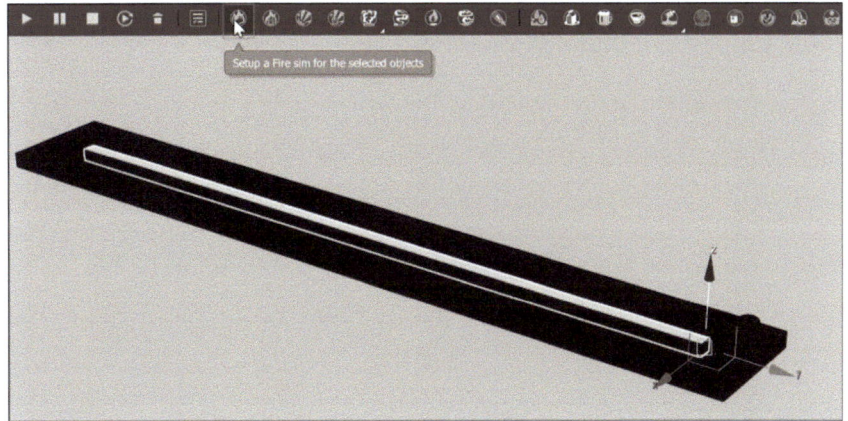

Figure 6.37

Choosing Setup a Fire sim for the selected objects from the PhoenixFD Toolbar.

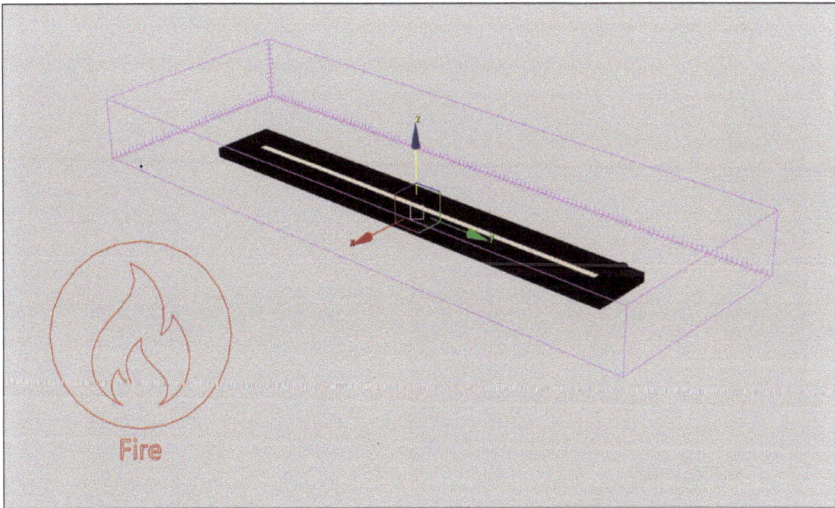

Figure 6.38

The Fire icon and the simulation box.

2. In the Dynamics rollout, locate the Time Scale setting:
   - Reduce the value to 0.5 to slow the flame movement (Figures 6.44).
   - Leaving this value 1 causes the fire to move fast.
3. Start a new simulation (Figure 6.45 and Video 6.3).
   Step 5. Adjust Flame Cooling.
   1. Delete the cache files, and reset to Frame 0.

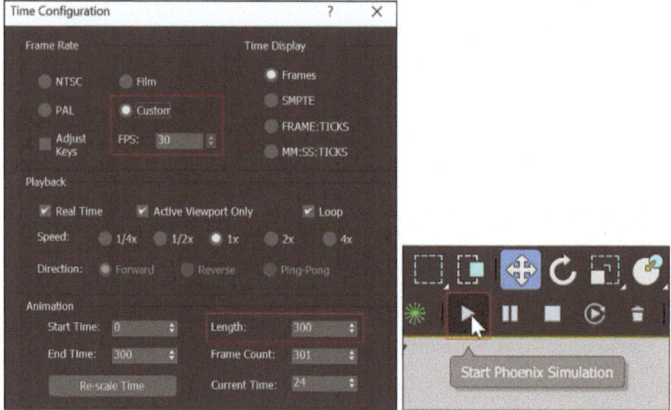

Figure 6.39

Setting the FPS to 30 and the Length to 300 Frames (left) and the Start Phoenix Simulation button (right).

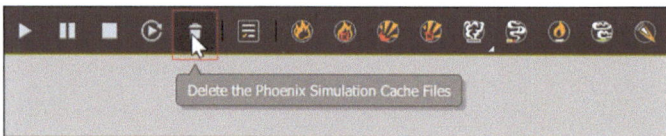

Figure 6.40

The Delete the Phoenix Simulation Cache Files command.

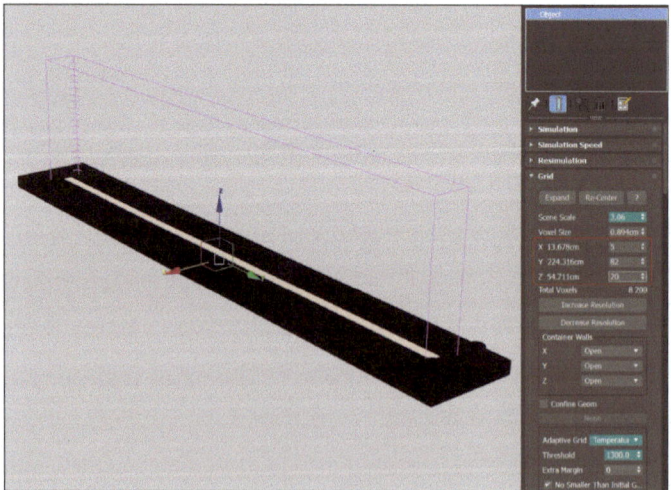

Figure 6.41

Updated size of the Grid.

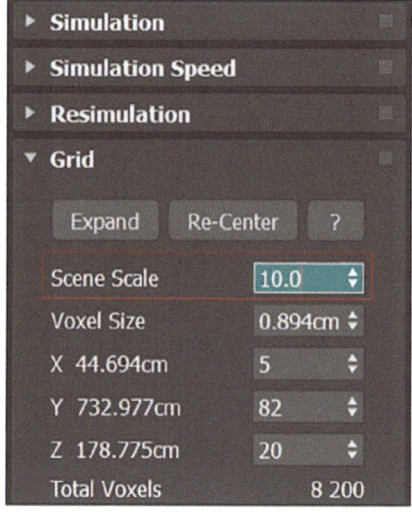

Figure 6.42

Scene Scale set to 10.

Figure 6.43

Screenshot of the fire simulation at Frame 300 with Scene Scale set to 10.

    2. In the Dynamics rollout, adjust the Cooling parameter:
- Lower values keep the flames hot and intense.
- Set the Cooling to 0.5 for softer, controlled flames (Figure 6.46).

    3. Start a new simulation (Figure 6.47 and Video 6.4).

Step 6. Adjust Gravity.

    1. Delete the cache files, and reset to Frame 0.

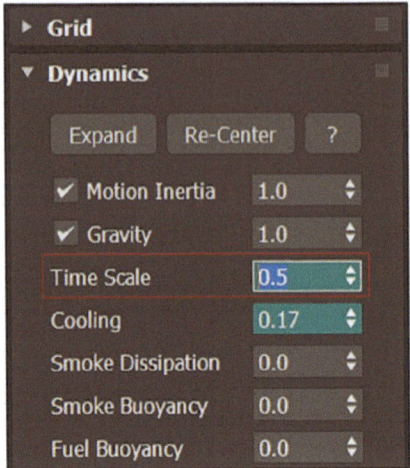

Time Scale set to 0.5.

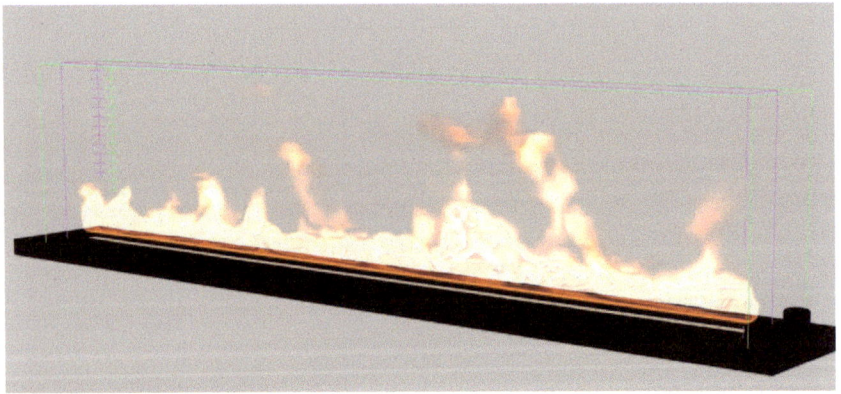

Figure 6.45

Screenshot of the fire simulation at Frame 300 with Time Scale set to 0.5.

   2. In the Dynamics rollout, modify the Gravity setting:
- Lower values create more chaotic and expansive flames.
- Set Gravity to 0.1 for a more natural flame spread (Figure 6.48).

   3. Start a new simulation (Figure 6.49 and Video 6.5).

Step 7. Adjust Outgoing Velocity.

   1. Delete the cache files, and reset to Frame 0.

   2. Select the fire icon in the viewport, and then go to the General rollout in the Modify panel.

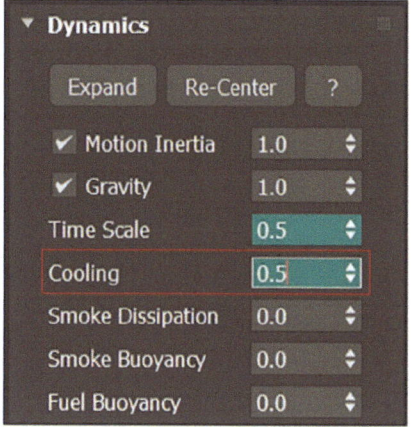

Figure 6.46

Cooling set to 0.5.

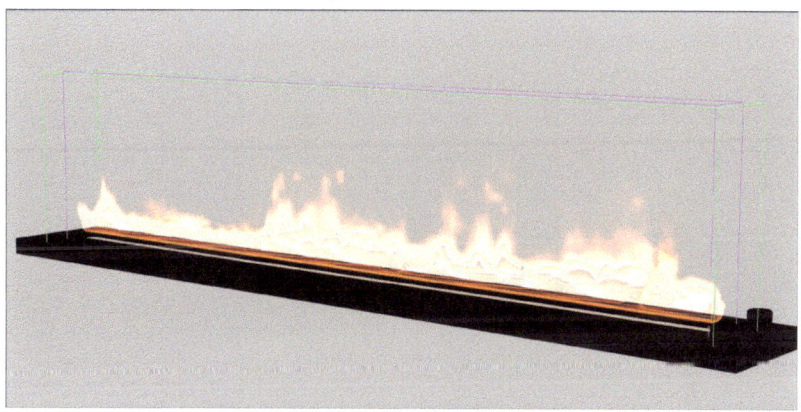

Figure 6.47

Screenshot of the fire simulation at Frame 300 with Cooling set to 0.5.

   3. Increase the Outgoing Velocity to elongate the flames:
- The higher this value, the more elongated the flames become.
- For example, set it from 12.943 to 30 cm (Figure 6.50).

   4. Simulate and review the updated flames (Figure 6.51 and Video 6.6).

Step 8. Adjust Quality.

   1. Delete the cache files, and reset to Frame 0.

   2. Increase the height of the grid in the Grid rollout.

   3. In the Dynamics rollout, increase the Fluidity Quality from 70 to 100 (Figure 6.52). This setting controls the level of detail and smoothness in the fluid simulation. Higher fluidity quality reduces flickering

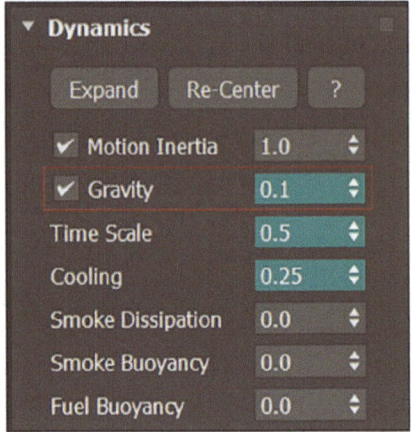

Figure 6.48

Set Gravity to 0.1.

Figure 6.49

Screenshot of the fire simulation at Frame 300 with Gravity set to 0.1.

or rough edges, making the simulation look more polished. Keep in mind that this may also increase simulation times, as the system processes more detailed calculations.

4. Start a new simulation (Figure 6.53 and Video 6.7).

Step 9. Final Adjustments.

1. Delete the cache files, and reset to Frame 0.
2. Refine parameters as needed:
   - Adjust Gravity to 0.15.
   - Lower Cooling to 0.25.

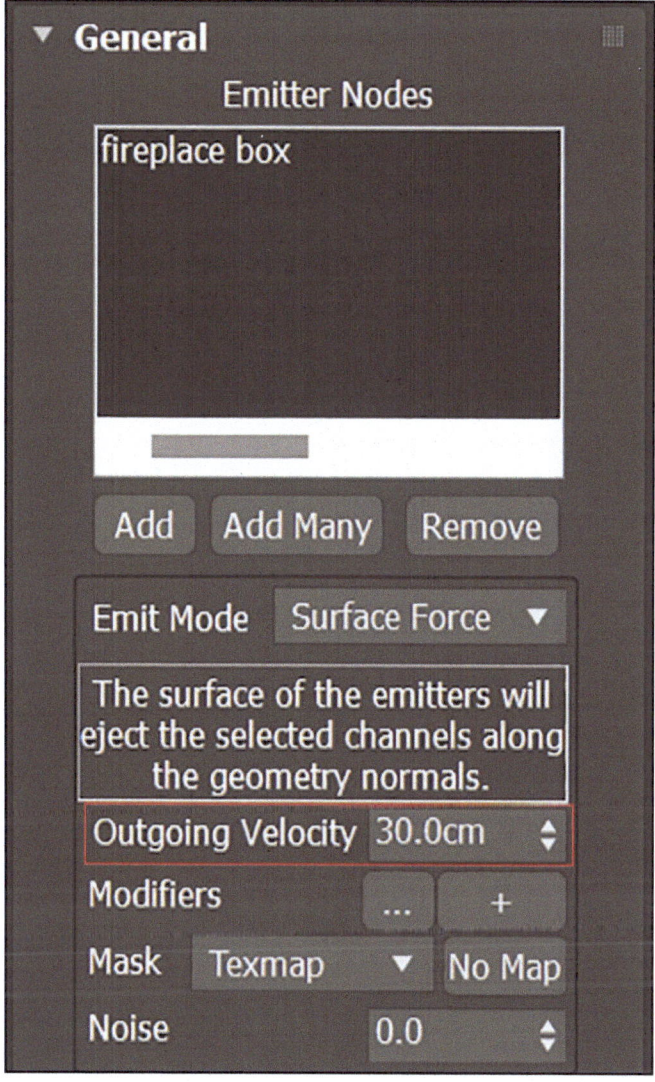

Figure 6.50

Set the Outgoing Velocity to 30 cm.

3. Double the calculation steps for higher accuracy (Figures 6.54 and 6.55).

4. In the Grid rollout, lower the Voxel Size for a more detailed simulation. The Voxel Size determines the resolution of the simulation grid – smaller voxels mean higher resolution, allowing for finer details in the fluid's movement and surface. By reducing the Voxel Size, you will achieve more realistic behavior, such as sharper flames

Figure 6.51

Screenshot of the fire simulation at Frame 300 with Outgoing Velocity set to 30cm.

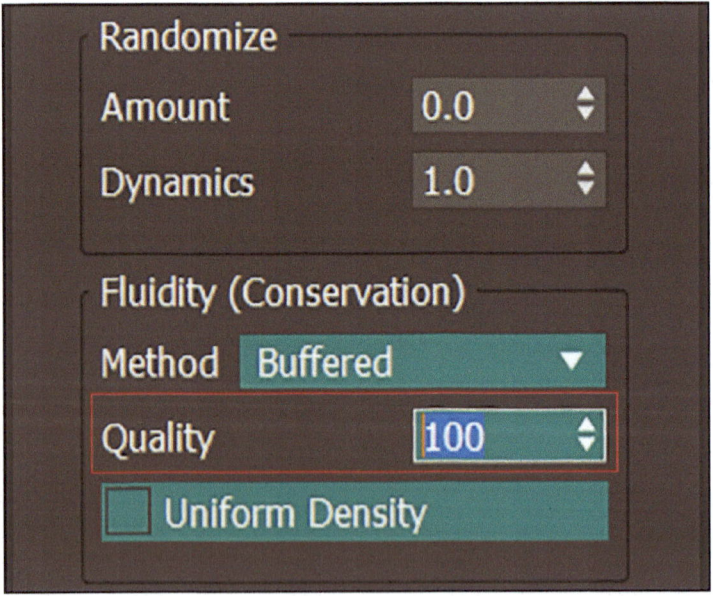

Figure 6.52

Set the Fluidity Quality to 100.

Figure 6.53

Screenshot of the fire simulation at Frame 300 with Quality set to 100.

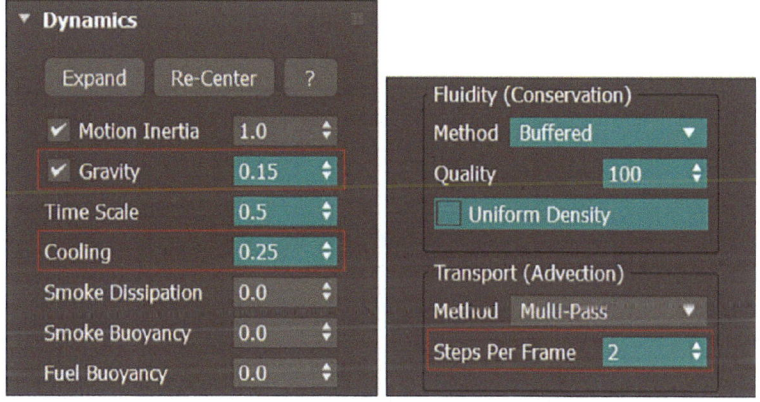

Figure 6.54

Adjusted value (left) and Steps Per Frame set to 2 (right).

and smoother movement. However, keep in mind that smaller voxels will increase both simulation time and memory usage, so it is important to find a balance based on your project's needs:

- The smaller the Voxel Size, the slower to calculate the simulation.
- Change the value to 0.5 cm, and do a new simulation (Figure 6.56).

5. Do a new simulation (Figure 6.57 and Video 6.8).

Figure 6.55

Screenshot of the fire simulation at Frame 300 with adjusted values and 2 Steps Per Frame.

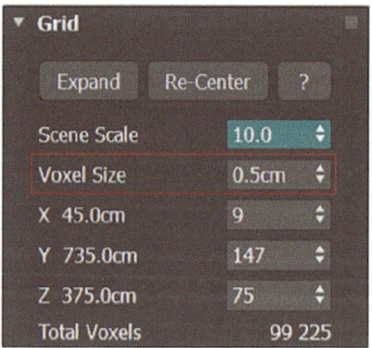

Figure 6.56

Voxel Size set to 0.5 cm.

Figure 6.57

Screenshot of the fire simulation at Frame 300 with Voxel Size 0.5.

Step 10. Render the Final Animation.
1. Before rendering, delete or hide the combustion box.
2. Produce a render at Frame 300 to see how the fire looks, before you render the full animation (Figure 6.58).
3. Choose to render all 300 frames or a specific range.

Experiment with the settings to further customize the flames to fit your scene and needs.

Figure 6.58

Render of the fire simulation at Frame 300.

Index

Note: *Italic* page numbers refer to figures.

adding keys *31, 32, 34*
animating depth of field (DOF) 62–67, *63–68*
animating modifiers 40
  bend modifier *40,* 40, *41*
  skew modifier 41, *42*
animating parameters 38
  height of the box *38,* 38
  hemisphere value of a sphere *39,* 39
animating the position of a camera 46, *48, 49*
  and camera target 49–54, *51–55*
animating the position of a light 80, *81*
  intensity of pendant 80–83, *82–85*
  intensity of pendant light 83–88, *85–87*
animating the position of the sun 93–94, *93–96*
animation
  box with auto key 30–32, *31*
  sphere with set key 32–34, *33–35*
  walkthrough 68–77, *70–79*
Animation and Time Controls 3
animation controls 21–24, *22*
animation settings 24, 29
  animation 28–29, *29*
  frame 24
  frame rate 24–26
  Playback settings 27–28

Time Display settings 26–27, *27*
Archive command 20, *20*
Autodesk 3ds Max 2025 1, *2,* 4
auto key
  animation box with 30–32, *31*
  vs. set key 30

Back up Time One Unit 21
bend modifier *40,* 40, *41*
box creation 9, *10*

camera animation 46, *47*
  Camera Navigation controls 55–56
  orbit camera 56, *56, 57*
  position of camera 46, *48, 49*
    and camera target 49–54, *51–55*
  settings 57
    animating depth of field 62–67, *63–68*
    camera clipping 60, *61, 62*
    camera focal length 58–60, *59–61*
camera clipping 60, *61, 62*
camera focal length 58–60, *59–61*
Camera Navigation controls 55–56
Chaos Cloud, rendering using *112,* 112–113, *113*
Chaos Corona Toolbar 3, *4*
Chaos Phoenix installation 123, *124*

color change, light 90–91, *90–92*
color temperature
    and light's color animation 88
    of pendants 88, *89*
Command Panel 3
Corona, rendering settings in 100–101, *101*
Current Frame Indicator 22
curves 43
    accessing the Curve Editor 43, *43*
    adjusting the Box's X-Position 44·
    right motion selection 45
    understanding ease in and ease out 44

double-cross, cursor conversion to 3, *4*

faucet water simulation 126–140, *126–142*
field-of-view (FOV) adjustments 55
File Archive dialog box 20
fireplace fire simulation 140, *144–156*
Forward Time One Unit 22
fps *see* frames per second (fps)
frame 24, 26, 27
frame rate 24–26
frames per second (fps) 24–29, *48, 82, 98,*
    142, 146

General menu 6

keyframes 29–30
    adjusting keyframes for timing 35, *36*
    animating a box with auto key
        30–32, *31*
    animating a sphere with set key 32–34,
        33–35
    auto key *vs.* set key 30
    copying keyframes for repeated motion
        35–36, *36*
    deleting keyframes from the timeline
        36–38, *37*

length, camera focal 58–60, *59–61*
light intensity animation 80, *81*
    intensity of pendant 80–83, *82–85*
    intensity of pendant light 83–88, *85–87*
light's color change 90–91, *90–92*

Main Toolbar 1
Menu bar 1

Name command 13, *13*
National Television System Committee
    (NTSC) 25
Navigation Controls 10

objects selection 13–14, *13, 14*
Object Type rollout 9
Open Mini Curve Editor 22
orbit camera 56, *56, 57*
Orbit command 6, *6*

Perspective viewports 8, *8,* 14, 18, *126, 127*
Per View Preference 6, *7*
Phase Alternating Line (PAL) 26
PhoenixFD Toolbar 123
Phoenix Simulation Cache Files
    command *146*
Playback settings 27–28
Point-of-View (POV) 6

Quick Export button 117

rendering settings
    in Corona 100–101, *101*
    in V-ray 101–106, *102–107*
rendering using Chaos Cloud *112,*
    112–113, *113*
rendering workflow 97–100, *98–100*
    combining images into a movie
        106–110, *107–111*
Render 2s button 116

Save As command 19
Save Selected command 20
Saving a Project 19
    Archive command 20, *20*
    Save As command 19
    Save Selected command 20
Select and Move command 14–15, *15*
Select and Place command 18, *18, 19*
Select and Rotate command 16, *16*
Select an Object command 13–14, *13, 14*
Select From Scene dialog box 13
set key
    animation sphere with 32–34, *33–35*
    vs. auto key 30
Shading menu 6
simple camera animation 46, *47*

Camera Navigation controls 55
orbit camera 56, *56*, *57*
position of camera 46, *48*, *49*
and camera target 49–54, *51–55*
settings 57
animating depth of field 62–67,
63–68
camera clipping 60, *61*, *62*
camera focal length 58–60, *59–61*
simulation
fireplace fire 140, *144–156*
water faucet 124–140, *125–142*
skew modifier 41, *42*
SMPTE format 26–27
Society of Motion Picture and Television
Engineers (SMPTE) format
26–27
sphere creation 11, *12*
standard primitives, create and modify
9–11, *9–11*
Status Bar 3
sunlight animation 93
position of sun 93–94, *93–96*

3ds Max Interface 1–3, *2*
Time Configuration dialog 24, *25*
Time Display settings 26–27, *27*
Timeline 22
Time Slider 3
Time Slider and Track Bar 21–22, *22*
Title bar 1

Topaz Labs 113–114
using Topaz video AI for frame
interpolation 120–122, *121*
using Topaz video AI to combine
images into video 118–119,
119, *120*
using Topaz video AI to upscale a
video 114–118, *114–118*
transform commands 14
Select and Move command 14–15, *15*
Select and Place command 18, *18*, *19*
Select and Rotate command 16, *16*
Select and Scale command 17–18, *18*

ViewCube 6
Viewport Navigation Controls 3, 4, 5, 6, *11*
Viewports 4–8
configuration *7*
menus *8*
Perspective *8*
V-Ray
rendering settings in 101–106, *102–107*
Toolbar 2, *4*, 112

walkthrough animation 68–77, *70–79*
water faucet simulation 124–140, *125–142*
Welcome Screen 1, *2*

Zoom Extends All Selected command 10,
11, *11*, *12*